Prairie View Elementary
W330 S6473 Highway E
North Prairie, WI 53153

WISCONSIN BIOGRAPHICAL DICTIONARY

HAMLIN GARLAND

WISCONSIN BIOGRAPHICAL DICTIONARY

—•—

**PEOPLE OF ALL TIMES AND ALL PLACES
WHO HAVE BEEN IMPORTANT TO THE HISTORY
AND LIFE OF THE STATE**

American Historical Publications, Inc.
725 Market Street
Wilmington, Delaware 19801

©

Copyright, 1991 by

American Historical Publications,Inc.

Library of Congress Cataloging-in-Publication Data

Wisconsin biographical dictionary : people of all times and all places who have been important to the history and life of the state.
    p.   cm.
  Includes index.
  ISBN 0-937862-67-3 : $69.00
  1. Wisconsin--Biography--Dictionaries.   I. American Historical Publications.
CT268.W57 1991
920.0775--dc20
                                     91-16466
                                         CIP

ADAMS, HENRY CULLEN, (1850-1906) a U. S. Representative from Wisconsin; born in Verona, Oneida County, N.Y., November 28, 1850; moved to Wisconsin in 1851 with his parents, who settled in Fort Atkinson, Jefferson County; attended the public schools, Albion Academy, and the University of Wisconsin at Madison; engaged in agricultural pursuits; member of the Wisconsin assembly 1883-1885; State superintendent of public property 1884-1890; engaged in work with the Wisconsin farmers' institutes 1887-1889; president of the Wisconsin Dairy Association and secretary of the State Horticultural Society; State dairy and food commissioner 1895-1902; elected as a Republican to the Fifty-Eighth and Fifty-ninth Congresses and served from March 4, 1903, until his death in Chicago, Ill., July 9, 1906; interment in Forest Hill Cemetery, Madison, Wis.

ALLIS, EDWARD PHELPS, (1824-1889), manufacturer, was born in Cazenovia, New York, May 12, 1824, son of Jere and Mary (White) Allis. He graduated from Union College in 1845 and moved to Milwaukee, Wisconsin the following year. There he formed a partnership with William Allen, a leather manufacturer, under the name of Allis & Allen. In 1854 he sold his interest in that business and entered into partnership with John P. McGregor, a real estate broker. With C. D. Nash and Mr. McGregor, Allis purchased the Reliance Iron Works in 1860, a small jobbing and repair shop. Allis bought his partners' interest later that year, and began the manufacture of all kinds of flour and saw mill machinery. In less than four years had increased the business from $30,000 to $100,000 annual income.

In seeking improvements in the grinding of flour he sent an expert to Europe in 1876 to study foreign methods, which resulted in his building the first all-roller mill in America in 1877. Its success was so pronounced that it was immediately followed by the introduction of the roller

1

system in all the larger milling centers of the United States. About this time he began to manufacture the celebrated Reynolds-Corliss engines, and a little later began building mining machinery. In its time the Edward P. Allis Co. was probably the largest manufacturer of pumping, blowing, electrical, tramway and all kinds of engines in the world, as well as the largest manufacturer of flour, sawmill and mining machinery. Twenty-eight acres in Milwaukee, employed about 2,500 men, and had an annual output of over $5,000,000 of finished product.

Allis was identified with the Milwaukee Advancement Association and was a Republican until 1877, when he affliated with the Greenback Party, of which he was the nominee for governor in that year. He made a study of finance, and wrote many valuable papers on the subject. In 1848 he was married to Margaret Watson, of Geneva, New York; they had twelve children. His son, William W., was president, and Charles Allis was secretary and treasurer of the company. Edward Allis died at his home in Milwaukee, Wisconsin, April 1, 1889.

ALLYN, STANLEY CHARLES (1891-1970), was a business executive who was president and chairman of the board of the National Cash Register Company.

Born in Madison, Wisconsin on July 20, 1891, he attended the University of Wisconsin, receiving an A.B. degree in 1913. In 1946, he was awarded an LL.D. degree.

He began his career at National Cash Register Company as an accountant, and worked his way up through the ranks as assistant comptroller, comptroller, treasurer, executive vice-president and general manager. He continued his ascent to director, becoming president in 1950, holding that post until 1957. He was chairman of the board, chief executive officer from 1957 to 1961. In 1962, he became chairman of the executive committee and in 1964, director emeritus.

After leaving the firm in 1970, he was director of various companies such as Dayco Corporation, Mead Corporation, Western Allegheny Railroad Company, and Master Consolidated, Inc.

Allyn was associated with numerous organizations, including: the National Conference of Christians and Jews; the Grand Central Art Galleries; the Thomas Alva Edison Foundation; the National Aviation Hall of Fame; and the Asia Foundation; among others.

He was given the Presidential Certificate of Merit, the U.S.N. Distinguished Public Service award, and was named Industrialist of the Year by the Society of Industrial Realtors.

Allyn was married to Helen Probasco Compton and the couple had three children. After she died, he remarried to Patricia von Krell Turnbull. He died on October 31, 1970.

AMECHE DON (ne Dominic Felix Ameche), is a stage, screen and television actor, as well as having been one of the participants in what was considered the golden age of radio.

Born in Kenosha, Wisconsin on May 31, 1908, he attended Columbia College in Dubuque, Iowa. Initially deciding on law as a career, Ameche took courses at other schools such as Georgetown University in Washington, D.C. and the University of Wisconsin in Madison.

While attending the latter school, Ameche gave up law for acting, something he had tried briefly after having a small role as a butler in the Broadway show *Jerry-For-Short*. It was in the 1930's that Ameche became involved in radio and began starring in such shows as *Grand Hotel*, *The First Nighter* and *The Chase and Sanborn Hour*. In a 1958 interview with the New York *Herald Tribune*, he described that era: "We went into everything all the way. In those days, the actors, the writers, everybody thought about nothing but the program. We worked hard at it...We had ten to fifteen writers....We cut no corners, believe me."

Perhaps his most well-known radio work was a series of husband and wife sketches, performed with Frances Langford on *The Drene Show*, entitled "The Bickerson's." After working successfully in films and on the stage, Ameche returned to radio in 1958, starring in *Don Ameche's Real Life Stories*, a weekly series.

His first movie role was in *Sins of Man*, and from then on, he made a series of pictures including: *Ladies in Love*, *Ramona*, *You Can't Have Everything*, *Alexander's Ragtime Band*, *Lillian Russell*, *Heaven Can Wait*, and what is considered his most famous movie, *The Story of Alexander Graham Bell*, a role that perpetrated numerous jokes about Ameche actually having been the one to invent the telephone.

Ameche made a few more pictures before deciding to move to New York and concentrate on stage work. His first role back on the boards was in the musical *Silk Stockings*, based on the Greta Garbo movie, *Ninotchka*. The musical, with songs by Cole Porter, was a success with both the audiences and the critics, the latter noting Ameche's fine singing voice. In the New York *Herald*

3

Tribune, Walter Kerr wrote: "Mr. Ameche is a decided find--if he can be called that at this juncture--for the musical comedy state. Possessed of a penetrating show-baritone that plugs a song handsomely, and of an easy-going authority that is never smug, he leers, scowls, smirks and furrows those pyramiding eyebrows with great good humor." New York's other stage critic, Brooks Atkinson of the New York *Times*, stated that Ameche was "the perfect musical comedy hero, crackling in style, deadpan, assured, sardonic."

Ameche continued doing stage work, appearing in *Holiday for Lovers*, *Goldilocks*, and *13 Daughters*. While in New York, he also began working in television, doing such shows as *High Button Shoes*, *Woodrow Wilson and the Unknown Soldiers*, General Motor's *Fiftieth Anniversary Show*, and *Climax*, in which he played Mafia don Albert Anastasia. He also became a regular panelist on *To Tell the Truth*, and the host of *International Showtime*.

He returned to the stage in 1967 in *I Married an Angel*, then continued working in such shows as *Henry Sweet Henry*, 1968; *The Odd Couple* (in the role of Oscar), 1972; *No, No, Nanette*, 1973; and *Never Get Smart with an Angel*, 1976.

He also gave films another try, starting with *A Fever in the Blood* in 1961, and continued with *Rings Around the World*, 1966; *Suppose They Gave a War and Nobody Came*, 1970; *The Boatniks*, 1970; *Cocoon* (for which he won his first and only Academy Award for best supporting actor), 1986; *Harry and the Hendersons*, 1987; and *Things Change*.

Ameche   has been married to his wife Honore Prendergast since 1932 and the couple have six children.

AMLIE, THOMAS RYUM, (1897-1973) a U. S. Representative   from Wisconsin; born on a farm near Binford, Griggs County, N.Dak., April 17, 1897; attended the public schools, Cooperstown (N.Dak.) High School, the University of North Dakota at Grand Forks, and the University of Minnesota at Minneapolis; was graduated from the law department of the University of Wisconsin at Madison in 1923; was admitted to the Wisconsin bar the same year and commenced the practice of law in Beloit, Wis.; moved to Elkhom, Wis., in 1927 and continued the practice of law; elected as a Republican to the Seventysecond Congress to fill the vacancy caused by the death of Henry Alien Cooper and served from October 13, 1931, to March 3, 1933; was an unsuccessful candidate for renomination in 1932 to the

Seventy-third Congress; elected as a Progressive to the Seventy-fourth and to the Seventy-fifth Congress (January 3, 1935-January 3, 1939); was not a candidate for renomination in 1938, but'was an unsuccessful Progressive candidate for nomination for United States Senator; nominated by President Franklin D. Roosevelt in 1939 to be a member of the Interstate Commerce Commission but subsequently requested that his name be withdrawn; resumed the practice of law; author; resided in Madison, Wis., until his death there August 22, 1973; cremated; ashes interred at Sunset Memory Gardens.

ANDREWS, ROY CHAPMAN (1884-1960), was a zoologist, explorer and author.

Born in Beloit, Wisconsin on January 26, 1884, he graduated from Beloit College in 1906. He soon moved to New York and became associated with the American Museum of Natural History. His first explorations began in 1908 at Vancouver Island and in Alaska.

He became a member of the crew of the *U.S.S. Albatross* and traveled to Borneo, the Celebes and the Dutch East Indies in order to study the habitats of whales. Six years later he decided to change his area of expertise to land explorations, investigating the terrain of Korea and Japan and becoming the leader of the Central Asian Expeditions, which covered Southwest China, Burma and Tibet. He continued his journeys, going to Northern China and Outer Mongolia, and from 1921 to 1930 he was part of a major expedition that cost $700,000 and involved forty men, eight cars and 150 camels.

It was money well spent as he and his assistants found important archeological treasures in the Gobi Desert such as skeletons of the oldest and largest known land mammals, the first known dinosaur eggs, as well as evidence of prehistoric life.

Andrews was head of the Museum of Natural History from 1935 to 1941 and he wrote several books concerning his work and travels, including: *Whale Hunting with Gun and Camera*, 1916; *Camps and Trails in China*, 1918; *Across Mongolian Plains*, 1921; *On the Trail of Ancient Man*, 1926; *The New Conquest of Central Asia*, 1932; *This Business of Exploring*, 1935; *Meet Your Ancestors*, 1945; and a three-part autobiography, *Under a Lucky Star*, 1943, *An Explorer Comes Home*, 1947, and *Beyond Adventure*.

Andrews was married twice and had two sons. He died in Carmel, California on March 11, 1960.

ASPIN, LESLIE, (1938-) a U. S. Representative from Wisconsin; born in Milwaukee, Milwaukee County, Wis., July 21, 1938; attended Milwaukee public schools; B.A., Yale University, 1960; M.A., Oxford University, England, 1962; Ph.D., economics, Massachusetts Institute of Technology, 1965; assistant professor of economics, Marquette University, Milwaukee, Wis., 1969-1970; economic adviser to the Secretary of Defense while serving in United States Army, 1966-1968; served in the United States Army, captain, 1966-1968; staff member to United States Senator William Proxmire in 1960, and was his campaign director in 1964 for reelection; staff assistant to Walter Heller, chairman of President Kennedy's Council of Economic Advisers, 1963; unsuccessful candidate for the office of Wisconsin State Treasurer; elected as a Democrat to the Ninety-second and to the eight succeeding Congresses (January 3, 1971-January 3, 1989); chairman, Committee on Armed Services (Ninety-ninth and One Hundredth Congresses); is a resident of East Troy, Wis.

B

BARDEEN, JOHN (1908-?), is an electrical engineer who is the co-creator of the transistor.

Born in Madison, Wisconsin on May 23, 1908, he attended the University of Wisconsin, receiving a B.S. degree in 1928 and an M.S. degree a year later. In 1930, he went to work as a geophysicist for the Gulf Research and Development Corporation, but in 1933, returned to school at Princeton University Graduate School, and was awarded a Ph.D. degree.

In 1938, he was appointed assistant professor in physics at the University of Minnesota, and when World War II began in 1941, he spent four years in Washington, D.C. as the principal physicist at the Naval Ordnance Laboratory.

After the War, he began working as a research physicist at Bell Telephone Laboratories, Inc. where he met the two men he would make history with, Dr. Walter H. Brattain and Dr. William Shockley. During that time, he said he was "primarily concerned with theoretical problems in solid state physics, including studies of semiconductor materials."

Bardeen was one of many who wanted to devise a better vacuum tube than the three-element type used at that time, which was bulky and had a short life. In 1948, he and his co-workers invented the "transistor," the name being an abbreviation of "transfer" and "resistor." It was described as a "point contact" device that "without vacuum, grid, plate, or cathode--and requiring only one-fiftieth the space of a vacuum tube and one-millionth the power--can perform most of its functions and even extend them," and as "a mighty mite...doing the work of the vacuum tube in nearly all phases of telephonics." In 1956, Bardeen, Brattain and Shockley were all give the Nobel Prize for Physics, for their "investigations on semiconductors and the discovery of the transistor effect." They were also given the Stuart Ballantine Medal of the Franklin Institute of the State of Pennsylvania in 1952, and "a major award in the field of physics," the John Scott Medal, in 1955. Bardeen was also given the Fritz London award, 1962, the Vincent Bendix award, 1964, the National Medal of Science, 1966, the Franklin Medal, 1975, and the Presidential Medal of Freedom in 1977.

Bardeen was the associate editor of the *Physical Review* from 1949 to 1952 and again in 1956. He is a member of the American Physical Society, the National Academy of Sciences and the American Association for the Advancement of Science.

He is married to Jane Maxwell and the couple have three children.

BARNEY, SAMUEL STEBBINS, (1846-1919) a U. S. Representative from Wisconsin; born in Hartford, Washington County, Wis., January 31, 1846; attended the public schools and Lombard University, Galesburg, Ill.; taught in the high school at Hartford for four years; studied law in West Bend, Wis.; was admitted to the bar in 1873 and commenced practice in West Bend; superintendent of schools of Washington County 1876-1880; delegate to the Republican National Convention at Chicago in 1884; unsuccessful candidate for election in 1884 to the Forty-ninth Congress; elected as a Republican to the Fiftyfourth and to the three succeeding Congresses (March 4, 1895-March 3, 1903); was not a candidate for renomination in 1902; appointed associate justice of the court of claims, Washington, D.C., in 1904 and served until 1919; died in Milwaukee, Wis., December 31, 1919; interment in Union Cemetery, West Bend, Washington County, Wis.

BARSTOW, WILLIAM AUGUSTUS (1813-1865), third governor of Wisconsin (1854-56), was born in Plainfield, Connecticut, September 13, 1813. He spent his boyhood at his home, attending school in winter and working on the farm in summer. At the age of sixteen he became a clerk in his brother's store at Norwich, Connecticut, but in 1834 moved to Cleveland, Ohio, where he was engaged for five years in the milling and forwarding business with another brother. Barstow then went to Wisconsin, established a flour mill at Prairieville, and filled the offices of postmaster and county commissioner. He subsequently settled in Madison, Wisconsin and in 1849 was elected Secretary of State by the Democratic party. Barstow was one of the first directors of the Milwaukee & Mississippi Railroad, and was instrumental in securing its charter. In 1853 he was elected governor and was installed in January of the following year.

During his term, the general corruption of state officials that characterized that period of Wisconsin history assumed unprecedented proportions, and his administration won an unenviable notoriety through a series of public scandals involving some of the highest state officers. It was then that the term "forty thieves" was applied to the lobbyists and officials who at the capital established headquarters know as "Monk's Hall," where some of the most shameful conspiracies to defraud the state were concocted. "Barstow and the balance," was another catch-phrase by which the opposition characterized the faction in power. It originated in a letter written by a printing contractor which contained this sentence: "We must get a good bid...even if we have to buy up Barstow and the balance." These scandals did not prevent Governor Barstow from being renominated by his party, and on being declared elected, he was installed for a second term in January, 1856. But his Republican opponent, Coles Bashford, contested the election, alleging fraud, and the Supreme Court decided against Governor Barstow. This was the first instance in the history of the country of the Supreme Court ousting a governor who had been duly installed in office, and seating a contestant.

In 1857 Governor Barstow moved to Janesville, and engaged in banking, but subsequently returned to the business of milling. When the Civil War began, he raised a cavalry regiment of which he was made colonel in February, 1862. In June following he was appointed provost marshal-general of Kansas, and he remained with his regiment in the southwest until February, 1863. While there he did creditable service, but, incapacitated by failing health, Barstow left field duty and spent the latter part of his military term sitting on courts-martial in St. Louis. On March 4, 1865, he was mustered out, and on March 13, he was brevetted Brigadier General of volunteers. Barstow died in Leavenworth, Kansas, December 14, 1865.

BASHFORD, COLES (1816-1878), fifth governor of Wisconsin (1856-58), was born near Cold Spring, New York, January 24, 1816. He received a classical education at Wesleyan University, now Genesee College, Lima, New York, and after spending seven years in the study of law, was admitted to the bar of the Supreme Court of New York, October 28, 1842. Bashford first practiced in Wayne County, New York, and in 1847 was elected District Attorney in that county as a Whig. In 1850 he moved to Oshkosh, Wisconsin, where he resumed his legal practice, and was

9

soon ranked with the eminent lawyers of the state. He entered political life in 1852, when he was elected to the state senate from Winnebago County. In 1854 he declined nomination of Congress, preferring re-election to his former office, and upon the organization of the Republican party in Pittsburg the same year, he joined the new party and became its first nominee for governor of Wisconsin in 1855. The contest was more than usually heated, and the Republicans were at first declared defeated, but Bashford succeeded in convicting the Democratic canvassers of doctoring the returns, and the election of his rival was set aside by the law courts. Bashford then entered the office of governor, March 25, 1856, and filled it for one term.

During his administration a public scandal that created much excitement resulted from the disposal of valuable land grants to railroads. An investigating committee reported in 1856 that managers of the La Crosse & Milwaukee Railroad Company had been "guilty of numerous and unparalleled acts of mismanagement, gross violation of duty, fraud and plunder," that stocks and bonds amounting to $175,000 had been distributed amoung thirteen senators and that thirty-nine members of the assembly had shared stocks and bonds valued at $355,000. It was also charged by the committee that the governor himself had been given bonds to the amount of $50,000 as a gratuity, but that the gift was made after the grant had been disposed of and was not the result of a previous understanding. The full account of these disreputable proceedings formed the subject of a volume called "Wisconsin Black Book."

In 1860 Governor Bashford was offered nomination for Congress, and declined, but spent the winter of 1862-63 in Washington, where he wielded an important outside influence on national affairs. After the organization of the territory of Arizona, he accompanied the newly appointed officers to that territory and assisted in the organization of the territorial government at Navajo Springs, being appointed Attorney General, December 29, 1863. He served as member and president of the territorial council of the first legislature, aiding it in framing the code of the territory; and as chairman of the judiciary committee in the second legislature. In 1866 Bashford was elected to represent Arizona in the 40th Congress, and at the close of his term, President Grant appointed him secretary of Arizona for four years. In 1871 Bashford was elected by the legislature to compile the session laws into one volume, and was reappointed by President Grant in 1873, holding office until 1876. Bashford then took up his residence in

Prescott, Arizona, where he spent the remainder of his life in retirement. Governor Bashford was married October 12, 1847, to Frances Adams, of Seneca Falls, New York. He died in Prescott, Arizona, April 25, 1878.

BERGER, VICTOR LUITPOLD, (1860-1929) a U. S. Representative from Wisconsin; born in Nieder Rebbach, Austria-Hungary, February 28, 1860; attended the Gymnasia at Leutschau and the universities at Budapest and Vienna; immigrated to the United States in 1878 with his parents, who settled near Bridgeport, Conn.; moved to Milwaukee, Wis., in 1880; taught school 1880-1890; editor of the Milwaukee Daily Vorwaerts 1892- 1898; editor of the Wahrheit, the Social Democratic Herald, and the Milwaukee Leader, being publisher of the last named at the time of his death; delegate to the People's Party Convention at St. Louis in 1896; one of the organizers of the Social Democracy in 1897 and of the Social Democratic Party in 1898, known since 1900 as the Socialist Party; unsuccessful candidate of the Socialist Party for election in 1904 to the Fifty-ninth Congress; elected a member of the charter convention of Milwaukee in 1907, and alderman at large in 1910; elected as a Socialist to the Sixty-second Congresses (March 4, 1911-March 3, 1913); presented credentials as a Member-elect to the Sixty-sixth Congress, but the House by a resolution adopted on November 10, 1919, declared him not entitled to take the oath of office as a U. S. Representative or to hold a seat as such; having been opposed to the entrance of the United States in the First World War and having written articles expressing his opinion on that question, he was indicted in various places in the Federal courts, tried at Chicago, found guilty, and sentenced by Judge Kenesaw M. Lanais in February 1919 to serve twenty years in the Federal penitentiary; this judgment was reversed by the United States Supreme Court in 1921, whereupon the Government withdrew all cases against him in 1922; his election to the Sixty-sixth Congress was unsuccessfully contested by Joseph P. Corner and the seat was declared vacant; presented credentials as a Member-elect to fill the vacancy caused by the action of the House and on January 10, 1920, the House again decided that he was not entitled to a seat in the Sixty-sixth Congress and declined to permit him to take the oath or

11

qualify as a U. S. Representative; Henry H. Bodenstab unsuccessfully contested this election, and on February 25, 1921, the House again declared the seat vacant; elected as a Socialist to the Sixty-eighth, Sixty-ninth, and Seventieth Congresses (March 4, 1923-March 3, 1929); unsuccessful candidate for reelection in 1928 to the Seventy-first Congress; resumed his editorial work; died in Milwaukee, Wis., August 7, 1929; interment in Forest Home Cemetery.

BLACK-HAWK, or KARA-ZHOUSEPT-HAH, (1767-1838), Indian chief was born in the present limits of Randolph County, Illinois, in 1767. He was the adopted brother of the chief of the Foxes, and although by birth a Pottawattomie, was brought up by the Sacs. He bore several names; at the time of the treaty at Prairie du Chien his name was *Hay-rayptshoan-sharp*, but later, when he was taken prisoner, it was *Muscata-mish-kia-kiak*. At the age of fifteen, already rated as a warrior, he was a leader amoung his people, and at twenty-one he became head chief of the Sacs.

His course from the start was one of opposition to the whites, and the assertion of the rights of his people even to lands sold by them. It is probable that his policy was shaped by the false information that the Americans were few and could not fight. In 1804 the Sacs and Foxes signed a treaty in St. Louis with General Harrison, in which, for an annuity of $1,000, they transferred to the United States their lands along the Mississippi River. Alleging that the chiefs were drunk at the time of signing, Black-Hawk for several years successfully resisted the ratification of its provisions. A second treaty was made, however, in 1816, he himself being a party, by which the cession of lands was completed. Seven years later the main body of both tribes migrated to their new reservation under the leadership of Keokuk, but Black-Hawk still remained behind.

In 1830 the chiefs of the Foxes were invited to a treaty at Prairie du Chien for a settlement of their difficulties with the Sioux. On the way to attend the treaty meeting, nine Foxes were killed by the Sioux, and next year a band of Sioux, within a mile of Prairie du Chien were attacked by Black-Hawk's party and twenty-eight were killed. The Americans demanded the murderers, but Black-Hawk refused to deliver them up.

By the treaty of 1830 the Sacs and Foxes had sold their country to the U.S. government. Black-Hawk had nothing to do with this sale, and the attempt to ratify it displeased him. When he heard, the following year, of his people having to move from his village, by the advice of the trader, to take up a residence elsewhere, he became the leader of those who were opposed to removal. The Sacs were then on the Rock River, and Black-Hawk agreed to deliver up their lead mines if allowed to hold their village. Their women and children, dispossessed, were on the banks of the Mississippi, without lodges, while the Sacs were camped on the west bank of that river. They decided to repossess their lands.

The whites agreed to let them plant together, but had secured the best grounds. The women were badly treated, but the Indians did not resort to retaliation until they were cheated out of their guns. Finally they were told not to come to the east side of the river, but Black-Hawk, refusing to obey, recrossed and took possession. Governor Reynolds declared Illinois invaded by hostile Indians, although they were only on U.S. lands, and six companies of regulars and 700 militia were ordered there under General Gaines. Black-Hawk met the general in council and declared he would not move, but when all the troops had arrived the Indians fled, returning only to take corn from their own lands. General Atkinson met them at Fort Madison, but they retreated up the Rock River to plant on the lands of Black-Hawk's son, the Prophet. Major Stillman followed them; a flag of truce was sent in, but its bearers were taken prisoners; five messangers sent by Black-Hawk were pursued and killed.

The war cry was then raised, and the Indians rushed on with guns, knives and tomahawks. Stillman ordered a retreat, which became a rout. Black-Hawk, with seventy men, had put to flight a detachment of 270. The chief then proceeded to Four Lakes, at the head of the Rock River. Atkinson pursued, and on June 18th, 3,000 whites brought face to face with 500 Indians were defeated after a difficult fight. General Scott was then ordered to the frontier with nine companies of artillery, but his troops were struck down with cholera. General Dodge fell on Black-Hawk's trail on Ouisconsin, and Black Hawk, deceived in his support, was forced to retreat, crossing the river in the night with much suffering and disaster.

At Blue Mounds, Dodge and Atkinson united forces in pursuit. While descending the Ouisconsin, Black-Hawk's forces were upset in their boats. Many drowned and others were captured. A steamboat overtook Black-Hawk's forces on August 1st, and the chief sent two white flags for surrender. A company of 150 of Black-Hawk's men, unarmed, approached the river, but the captain of the boat fired into them. The next morning General Atkinson's whole army was upon them, and Black-Hawk's forces were defeated and driven into the river, to their total destruction.

Black-Hawk again escaped, but this fight ended the war. The Sioux, with 100 men, pursued the flying Sacs, and murdered another 120 of them. Two young Winnebagoes brought Black-Hawk into camp, dressed in white deer skin clothes made for him by squaws. When taken before the commander he said: "You have taken me prisoner; I am grieved. I tried to bring you into ambush. I saw my evil day was at hand. Black-Hawk's heart is dead, but he can stand torture; he is no coward—he is an Indian who fought for his squaws, against those who came to cheat. You know the cause of this war, and you ought to be ashamed of it. We looked up to the Great Spirit. Farewell, my nation".

Black-Hawk, with eleven chiefs and fifty warriors, was landed at the lower rapids. His two sons, Prophet and Naopope, and five principal warriors, were given up as hostages to be held during the pleasure of the president, at Jefferson Barracks, Missouri. Black-Hawk was then about 63 years of age. Not a chief by birth, he had acquired his position by bravery and wisdom. In his interview with President Jackson, he said, with true dignity: "I am a man; and you are another." The president directed that articles of dress intended for his party be exhibited and distributed, and commanded him to go to Fort Monroe. Black-Hawk replied: "If I had not struck for my people they would have said I was a woman. Black-Hawk expects to return to his people." The president replied: "When all is quiet you may return," and assured him that his women should be protected.

On June 5, 1833, they were set free. President Jackson again met Chief Black-Hawk in Baltimore, and all along the return route crowds greeted him. In New York he visited the Seneca Reservation. He arrived at Fort Armstrong in August, 1833. Indians met him there with bands of music. Keokuk was then the acknowledged chief of his tribe, and Black-Hawk, declaring that he would not conform to anyone, departed in silence, downcast and broken. Black-Hawk died in Des Moines, Iowa, October 3, 1838. He was buried according to the custom of the Sacs; his body seated on the ground; his cane between his knees, grasped in his hands, with slabs or rails then piled about him.

BLAINE, JOHN J. (1875-1934), twenty-fourth governor of Wisconsin, was born in Wingville, Wisconsin on May 4 1875, the son of James and Elizabeth (Brunstadt Johnson) Blaine. He attended Valparaiso University in Indiana where he studied law and graduated in 1896. He was admitted to the Wisconsin Bar and began to practice in Montfort. After a year, he moved to Boscobel. He was elected Mayor of that city for four successive terms and also served as county supervisor for four years. In 1904, he married Anna McSpaden. They had one adopted daughter, Helen.

In the Republican State Conventions of 1902 and 1904, Blaine supported La Follette for governor. Blaine was elected to the State Senate in 1908. He ran for governor in 1914, but lost the election. In 1918, he was elected Attorney General and served for two years. He became Governor of Wisconsin in 1920, an office he held for three terms. During his administration, Blaine was a strong proponent of tax reform. He presented himself as the "Economy Governor" and strived to reduce state expenditures. In 1926, he was elected to the U.S. Senate. He served a single term, then was appointed director of the Reconstuction Finance Corportation by President Roosevelt. Blaine died suddenly of pneumonia on April 16, 1934.

BLANCHARD, GEORGE WASHINGTON, (1884-1964) a U. S. Representative from Wisconsin; born in Colby, Marathon County, Wis., January 26, 1884; attended the graded and high schools; was graduated from the University of Wisconsin at Madison in 1906 and from its law department in 1910; was admitted to the bar in 1910 and commenced practice in Edgerton, Rock County, Wis.; city attorney of Edgerton from 1912 until his resignation in 1932, having been elected to Congress; member of the State assembly 1925-1927; served in the State senate 1927-1933; elected as a Republican to the Seventythird Congress (March 3, 1933-January 3, 1935); was a candidate for renomination, but withdrew after being nominated; practiced law in Edgerton, Wis., until his death there October 2, 1964; interment in Fassett Cemetery.

BODE, CARL (1911-?), is an educator and a writer.

Born in Milwaukee, Wisconsin on March 14, 1911, he received a Ph.B. degree from the University of Chicago in 1933, an M.A. degree from Northwestern University in 1938, and attained his Ph.D. degree in 1941.

He first taught at Milwaukee Vocational School from 1933 to 1937. After finishing his schooling, he became assistant professor of English at the University of California, Los Angeles for one year beginning in 1946. In 1947, he

15

became a professor in English at the University of Maryland, College Park, where he stayed until 1982. He was a visiting professor at such schools as California's Institute of Technology, Claremont College, Northwestern University, the University of Wisconsin and Stanford.

He was the executive secretary of the American Civilization program at the University of Maryland from 1950 to 1957 and beginning in the latter year, took a leave of absence from the school to serve as a cultural attache at the American Embassy in London. During those two years, he was the chairman of the United States Educational Commission, also based in the U.K.

He has written numerous books, some of which include: (poems) *The Sacred Seasons*, 1953; *The Man Behind You*, 1959; *Practical Magic*, 1981; (books) *The American Lyceum*, 1956; *The Anatomy of American Popular Culture*, *1840-1861*, 1959 (republished as Antebellum Culture in 1970); *The Half-World of American Culture*, 1965; *Mencken*, 1969, 73, re-issue 86; and *Maryland: A Bicentennial History*, 1978.

He also wrote a newspaper column entitled *Highly Irregular* in 1974, and edited several different books, such as: *Collected Poems of Henry Thoreau*, 1943; *The Portable Thoreau*, 1947; *American Life in the 1840's*, 1967; *The Selected Journals of Henry David Thoreau*, 1967; *The Best of Thoreau's Journals*, 1971; and *Ralph Waldo Emerson, A Profile*, 1969; among many others.

Bode has been awarded various fellowships, including the Ford Foundation fellow, 1952-53; the Newberry Library fellow, 1954; and the Guggenheim Foundation fellow, 1954-55. He served with the United State Army during 1944-45.

He was married to the late Margaret Lutze and the couple had three children. He remarried to Charlotte Smith.

BOILEAU, GERALD JOHN, (1900-) a U. S. Representative from Wisconsin; born in Woodruff, Oneida County, Wis., January 15, 1900; moved to Minocqua, Oneida County, Wis., in 1909; attended the public and high schools; during the First World War enlisted in the United States Army on February 25, 1918, as a private in the Eleventh Field Artillery, Battery D, and was honorably discharged as a corporal on July 16, 1919, having served twelve months overseas; was graduated from the law department of Marquette University, Milwaukee, Wis., LL.B., 1923; was admitted to the bar the same year and commenced practice in

Wausau, Marathon County, Wis.; served as district attorney of Marathon County, Wis., 1926 1931; delegate to the Republican National Convention in 1928; elected as a Republican to the Seventy-second and Seventy-third Congresses and as a Progressive to the Seventy-fourth and Seventy-fifth Congresses (March 4, 1931 January 3, 1939); unsuccessful candidate for reelection in 1938 to the Seventy-sixth Congress and for election in 1940 to the Seventy-seventh Congress; resumed the practice of law; elected circuit judge of the sixteenth judicial circuit of Wisconsin in 1942; reelected in 1945, 1951, 1957, and again in 1963 for a six-year term; retired in 1970; appointed to serve as temporary circuit judge in Milwaukee County in 1970, for an unexpired term ending in 1974; resided in Wausau, Wis.,

BOLLES, DONALD F. (1928-1976), was an investigative reporter who was murdered while working on a story.

Born in Milwaukee, Wisconsin, he graduated from Beloit College in 1950. He began his career in 1953 as a sports editor and rewriter for the Associated Press. He became an investigative reporter for the *Arizona Republic* in 1962 and worked in that capacity until his death.

During his career he wrote expose's on various fraud schemes involving companies such as Western Growth Capital Corporation, and Emprise Corporation, and also uncovered the accepting of kickbacks in the state tax and corporation commissions of Arizona as well as a conflict-of-interest scandal in the state legislature.

Bolles' last years as an investigative reporter were filled with mounting frustration due to the apparent disinterest by the police, the political leaders, and even the public in the corruption he was writing about, once describing the scenario as the "official gutlessness in town." His managing editor at the *Arizona Republic* concurred, saying: "In 14 years of trying, Don Bolles was not able to make a sufficient dent on the Arizona criminal scene to prevent his own murder."

Bolles eventually asked to be reassigned to another bureau, deciding to give up investigative reporting entirely. Jon Bradshaw, quoted the *Republic's* city editor, who described the frustration Bolles was going through: "I've seen the same things happen to many reporters in many places. After about ten years of investigative work it gets to you and you need a break. Don worked *all* the time, including weekends. Investigative reporting has been glamorized recently. There's nothing glamorous about it.

You get untold harrassment from lawyers, a lot of nasty rumors spring up around you, and you get enormous pressure from your family. Add to that the frustration of nothing ever happening and all of a sudden you want to lead a normal life.''

However, Bolles was willing to follow one more lead after a man called him claiming he could provide the reporter with information concerning top political figures involved in illegal land deals. When Bolles arrived at the meeting place agreed upon, he received a call from the informant telling him that he couldn't make it. Bolles returned to his car and drove a short distance before his car was blown up by a bomb that was detonated by a remote control. He clung to life for eleven days, finally succumbing on June 13, 1976.

Before he died he was able to provide the authorities with the name of John Adamson, also mentioning that the Mafia was involved. Adamson was found, and pleaded guilty to second-degree murder. He received a lesser sentence of twenty years and two months in exchange for information he gave to authorities concerning others who wanted to have Bolles killed. By the time it was all over, two other men were tried and convicted for Bolles' murder, both receiving the death sentence.

Bolles was nominated for a Pulitzer Prize in 1965, and was named reporter of the year in 1974 by the Arizona Press Club. He also received the John Peter Zenger Award from the Arizona Newspaper Association after his death.

Bolles was married twice and had seven children.

BOLLES, STEPHEN (1866-1941) attended the public schools; was graduated from the State Normal School of Pennsylvania at Slippery Rock, Pa., in 1888 and from the law department of Milton College, Milton, Wis.; served as reporter correspondent, managing editor, and publisher of newspapers in Ohio, Pennsylvania, and New York, 1S93-1901; chairman of the congressional committee of the Eleventh Ohio District and secretary of the Republican city committee of Toledo in 1894; chairman of the congressional committee of the seventy-sixth Pennsylvania District and secretary of the Pennsylvania Republican League of Clubs in 1896; superintendent of the press department of the Pan American Exposition at Buffalo, N.Y., in 1901; managing editor of the Buffalo (N.Y.) Enquirer in 1902 and 1903; superintendent of graphic arts of the St. Louis Exposition 1903-1905; director of publicity of the Jamestown Exposition in 1907; engaged as a special writer and also in private business, including the brokerage business, in Atlanta, Ga., 1907-1919; moved to Janesville, Wis., in 1920 and again engaged as a newspaper editor until elected to Congress; delegate to the Republican National Convention in 1928; elected as a Republican to the Seventy-sixth and Seventy-seventh Congresses and served from January 3, 1939, until his death in Washington, D.C.; interment in Oak Hill Cemetery, Janesville, Wis.

BOLLING, RICHARD WALKER, (1916-) (great-great-grandson of John Williams Walker and great-great-nephew of Percy Walker), a U. S. Representative from Missouri; born in New York City, attended grade schools and Phillips Exeter Academy, Exeter, N.H.; at the age of fifteen, upon his father's death, returned to his home in Huntsville, Ala.; B.A., 1937, M.A., 1939, University of the South, Sewanee, Tenn.; graduate studies, Vanderbilt University, Nashville, Tenn., 1939-1940; taught at Sewanee Military Academy in 1938 and 1939; served as assistant to the head of the Department of Education, Florence State Teachers College, in Alabama, in 1940; educational administrator by profession; entered the United States Army as a private in April 1941, and served until discharged as a lieutenant colonel in July 1946, with four years' overseas service in Australia, New Guinea, Philippines, and in Japan as assistant to chief of staff to General MacArthur; awarded the Legion of Merit and Bronze Star Medal; veterans' adviser at the University of Kansas City in 1946 and 1947; elected as a Democrat to the Eighty-first and to the sixteen succeeding Congresses (January 3, 1949-January 3, 1983); chairman, Select Committee on Committees of the House (Ninety-third Congress), Joint Economic Committee (Ninty-fifth Congress); Committee on Rules (Ninety-sixth and Ninety-seventh Congresses); was not a candidate for reelection in 1982; is a resident of Crumpton, Md.

BOND, CARRIE JACOBS (1862-1946), was a composer and author.
  Born in Janesville, Wisconsin on August 11, 1862, she came from a musical family which included a distant cousin, John Howard Payne who wrote "Home, Sweet Home." She showed her proclivity for music at an early age, playing piano at four years old. She later took years of piano lessons.
  She married young as well, at the age of eighteen, and had one child, a son. She divorced after seven years of

marriage, and two years later, married Frank Lewis Bond who was a doctor. The couple resided at Iron River, a town inhabited mostly by miners and loggers. Her husband died in 1895 after falling on some ice and soon after, she moved to Chicago where she ran a rooming house and also hand-painted china in order to support her son.

During her second marriage she had written two songs, "Is My Dolly Dead?" and "Mother's Cradle Song," both of which had been published. She continued to write songs, in the beginning, only sharing them with close friends. Eventually those friends, some of whom were professional singers, helped introduce her work to the public. Jessie Bartlett Davis, a contralto, helped her publish a collection of tunes, *Seven Songs as Unpretentious as the Wild Rose*, which included "Just a Wearyin' for You," and "I Love You Truly." Her other high-powered friends included composer Ethelbert Nevin, actress Margaret Anglin, and writer/craftsman Elbert Hubbard. She was even extended an invitation from President Roosevelt to sing at the White House.

Her most famous song was "A Perfect Day," a song she wrote in 1910, inspired by a particularly spectacular sunset she had witnessed. By 1920, the song had sold over five million copies, and had been given sixty various arrangements.

She continued writing songs into her 80's, although many were not published. As times were changing, the war brought a type of cynicism that began to preclude the sweetness of Bond's songs and her type of lyrics began to go out of style.

In 1928, she lost her son when he took his own life during a severe depression he was experiencing. She wrote two books, one autobiographical, *The Roads of Melody* (1927), and one a collection of her own personal philosophies entitled *The End of the Road* (1940). She also wrote articles for several periodicals.

She died on December 28, 1946 at the age of eighty-five. At Forest Lawn Memorial Park where she is buried, she has a bronze plaque in the Memorial Court of Honor, which has a tribute given by Herbert Hoover concerning her "heart songs that express the loves and longings, sadness and gladness of all peoples everywhere."

BOUCK, JOSEPH (1788-1858) (uncle of Gabriel Bouck), a U. S. Representative from New York; born on Bouck's Island, near Fultonham, Schoharie County, N.Y., July 22, 1788; attended the rural schools of his native county; engaged in agricultural pursuits for many years in Schoharie County until his change of residence to Middleburgh; served as inspector of turnpike roads in Schoharie County in 1828; elected as a Jacksonian to the Seventy-second Congress (March 4, 1831-March 3, 1833); resided in Middleburgh, N.Y. until his death on March 30, 1858; interment in his son's plot in Middleburgh Cemetery.

BRAUER, JERALD CARL (1921-?), is an historian and an educator.

Born in Fond du Lac, Wisconsin on September 16, 1921, he received an A.B. degree from Carthage College in 1943, a B.D. degree from Northwestern Lutheran Theological Seminary in 1945 and a Ph.D. from the University of Chicago in 1948. In 1951, he became an ordained minister of the United Lutheran Church of America.

Brauer was an instructor in church history and history of Christian thought at the Union Theological Seminary in New York from 1948 to 1950. During the latter year he became assistant professor at the University of Chicago and in 1954, became associate professor. Starting in 1959, he became professor of the history of Christianity, becoming a Naomi Shenstone Donnelley Professor in 1960.

He also was dean of the federated theological faculty from 1955 to 1960, dean of Divinity School from 1960 to 1970 and president of the International House beginning in 1973.

Brauer was a visiting professor for one summer at the University of Frankfort in 1961, and traveled to universities throughout Japan as a guest lecturer during 1966.

Some of his writings include: *Protestantism in America*, 1953; *Luther and the Reformation*, 1953; *Basic Questions for the Christian Scholar*, 1954; and *Images of Religion in America*, 1967. He has been editor of various works such as: *The Future of Religions*, 1966; *My Travel Diary*, 1936; *Religion and the American Revolution*, 1976; and *Westminster Dictionary of Church History*, 1971.

He has also contributed articles to various religious periodicals, as well as providing information to *American People Encyclopedia* and *Encyclopaedia Britannica*.

He is married to Muriel N. Nelson and the couple have three children.

BRICKNER, GEORGE H., (?-1904) a U. S. Representative from Wisconsin; born in Anspach, Bavaria, Germany, January 21, 1834; immigrated to the United States in 1840 with his parents, who settled in Seneca County, Ohio; attended the public schools; engaged in mercantile pursuits in Tiffin, Ohio, 1850-1855; moved to Cascade, Wis., in 1855 and again engaged in mercantile pursuits; operated a flour mill until 1868, when he engaged in the manufacture of woolens at Sheboygan Falls, Wis.; established a glass factory in Tiffin, Ohio, in 1889; elected as a Democrat to the Fifty-first, Fifty-second, and Fifty-third Congresses (March 4, 1889-March 3, 1895); chairman, Committee on Expenditures in the Department of the Treasury (Fifty-second Congress); was not a candidate for reelection in 1894 to the Fifty-fourth Congress; lived in retirement in Sheboygan Falls, Sheboygan County, Wis., until his death on August 12, 1904; interment in St. Mary's Cemetery.

BROPHY, JOHN CHARLES, (1901-1976) a U. S. Representative from Wisconsin; born in Eagle, Walworth County, Wis.; attended the public and parochial schools of Milwaukee, Wis.; was graduated from St. Patrick's and Marquette Academy; enlisted in the United States Navy during the First World War and served as a seaman from August 1919 until honorably discharged in May 1921; worked as a mechanic 1922-1938; alderman of the city of Milwaukee from April ' 1939 to December 1946; unsuccessful candidate for election in 1942 to the Seventy-Eighth Congress; elected as a Republican to the Eightieth Congress (January 3, 1947-January 3, 1949); unsuccessful candidate for reelection in 1948 to the Eighty-first Congress and for election in 1950 to the Eightysecond Congress; engaged in sales and public relations until retirement in 1969; resided in Milwaukee, Wis., where he died; interment in Mount Olivet Cemetery.

BROWN, WEBSTER EVERETT, (1851-1929) a U. S. Representative from Wisconsin; born near Peterboro village, Madison County, N.Y., July 16, 1851; moved with his parents to Wisconsin in 1857; resided for a time in Newport, Columbia County, and then in Hull and Stockton, Portage County; attended the common schools; completed a preparatory course at Lawrence University, Appleton, Wis., and later, in 1870, a business course at the Spencerian Business College, Milwaukee, Wis.; was graduated from the University of Wisconsin at Madison in 1874; engaged in the logging and lumber business at Stevens Point, Wis., in 1875; moved to Rhinelander, Oneida County, Wis., in 1882 and continued in the logging and lumber business; also engaged in manufacture of paper; mayor of Rhine lander in 1894 and 1895; elected as a Republican to the Fifty-seventh, Fifty-Eighth, and Fifty-ninth Congresses (March 4, 1901-March 3, 1907); chairman, Committee on Mines and Mining (Fifty-Eighth and Fifty-ninth Congresses); was not a candidate for renomination in 1906; resumed his former business and manufacturing pursuits in Rhinelander, Wis.; died in Chicago, Ill., while on a visit for medical treatment, December 14, 1929; interment in Forest Home Ceme tery, Rhinelander, Wis.

BURCHARD, SAMUEL DICKINSON, (1836-1901) a U. S. Representative from Wisconsin; born in Leyden, N.Y., July 17, 1836; moved with his father to Beaver Dam, Wis., in 1845; attended Madison (now Colgate) University, Hamilton, N.Y.; engaged in the wool manufacturing business in Beaver Dam; during the Civil War entered the Union Army as a lieutenant in the I' Missouri Militia; appointed assistant quartermaster of United States Volunteers with the rank of captain; was stationed at New York; was mustered out with the rank of major; member of the Wisconsin senate 1872-1874; elected as a Democrat to the Forty-fourth Congress (March 4, 1875- March 3, 1877); engaged in agricultural pursuits; died in Greenwood, Wise County, Tex., September 1, 1901; interment in Greenwood Cemetery.

BURKE, MICHAEL EDMUND, (1863-1954) a U. S. Representative from Wisconsin; born at Beaver Dam, Dodge County, Wis., October 15, 1863; attended the public schools and was graduated from the Wayland Academy at Beaver Dam in 1884; studied law at the University of Wisconsin at Madison in 1886 and 1887; was admitted to the bar in 1888 and commenced practice at Beaver Dam; town clerk 1887-1889; member of the State assembly 1891-1893; served in the State senate 1895-1899; city attorney of Beaver Dam 1893-1908; delegate to the Democratic National Convention in 1904; elected mayor of Beaver Dam and served from 1908 to 1910; elected as a Democrat to the Sixty-second, Sixty-third, and Sixty-fourth Congresses (March 4, 1911-March 3, 1917); unsuccessful candidate for reelection in 1916; died at Beaver Dam, Wis., December 12, 1918; interment in St. Patrick's Cemetery.

BURKE, RAYMOND HUGH, U. S. Representative from Ohio; born in Nicholsville, Clermont County, Ohio, November 4, 1881; attended Jackson School; worked on a farm and in the village while studying to teach in rural schools; taught at Pendleton School near Point Pleasant in 1899 and 1900; student at Oberlin Academy and College 1900-1905; was graduated from the University of Chicago in 1906; taught in Miami University at Oxford, Ohio, 1906-1915; personnel and employment manager 1918-1923; secretary-treasurer of an automobile agency 1923-1926; special representative for an insurance company at Hamilton, Ohio, 1926-1954; mayor of Hamilton 1928-1940 and councilman 1928-1942; member of the State senate 1942-1946; elected as a Republican to the Eightieth Congress (January 3, 1947-January 3, 1949); unsuccessful candidate for reelection in 1948 to the Eighty-first Congress; lecturer in the finance department of Miami University in 1949 and 1950; died in Hamilton, Ohio, August 18, 1954; interment in Greenwood Cemetery.

C

CANNON, RAYMOND JOSEPH, (1894-1951) a U. S. Representative from Wisconsin; born in Ironwood, Gogebic County, Mich., August 26, 1894; his parents having died when he was six months old, he spent his early life in a home for dependent children; attended the public schools; taught school at Minocqua, Wis., in 1910 and 1911; professional baseball player 1908-1922; attended the law department of Marquette University, Milwaukee, Wis., for two years; was admitted to the bar in 1914 and commenced practice in Milwaukee; unsuccessful candidate for election as associate justice of the Wisconsin Supreme Court in 1930; elected as a Democrat to the Seventy-third, Seventy-four'th, and Seventy-fifth Congresses (March 4, 1933-January 3, 1939); chairman, Committee on Revision of the Laws (Seventy-fourth and Seventy-fifth Congresses); was an unsuccessful candidate for renomination as a Democrat and for reelection in 193S as an Independent to the Seventy-sixth Congress; resumed the practice of law; unsuccessful candidate for the Democratic gubernatorial nomination in 1940 and 1942 and for the Democratic nomination for Congress in 1944; died in Milwaukee, Wis., November 25, 1951; interment in Holy Cross Cemetery.

CARY, WILLIAM JOSEPH, (1865-1934) a U. S. Representative from Wisconsin; born in Milwaukee, Wis., March 22, 1865; educated in the public schools and St. John's Academy; was left an orphan at the age of eleven, when he became a messenger boy; studied telegraphy and was employed as a telegraph operator 1883-1895; engaged in the brokerage business 1895-1905; elected a member of the board of aldermen of Milwaukee in 1900 and was reelected in 1902 for the term ending in 1904; served as sheriff of Milwaukee County 1904-1906; elected as a Republican to the Sixtieth and to the five succeeding Congresses (March 4, 1907-March 3, 1919); unsuccessful candidate for renomination in 1918 to the Sixty-Sixth Congress; served as county clerk of Milwaukee County 1921-1933; died in Milwaukee, Wis., January 2, 1934; interment in Calvary Cemetery.

CASWELL, LUCIEN BONAPARTE, (1827-1919) a U. S. Representative from Wisconsin; born in Swanton, Franklin County, Vt., November 27, 1827; moved to Wisconsin in 1837 with his parents, who settled near Lake Koshkonong, in Rock County; attended the common schools, Milton Academy, and Beloit College; studied law; was admitted to the bar in 1851 and commenced practice in Fort Atkinson, Wis.; district attorney of Jefferson County in 1855 and 1856; served on the local school board for nearly sixty-five years; organized the First National Bank of Fort Atkinson in 1863, the Northwestern Manufacturing Cc. in 1866, and the Citizens' State Bank in 1885; member of the State assembly in 1863, 1872, and 1874 ; during the Civil War served as commissioner of the second district board of enrollment from September 1863 to May 5, 1865; delegate to the Republican National Convention in 1868; elected as a Republican to the Forty-fourth and to the three succeeding Congresses (March 4, 1875-March 3, 1883); unsuccessful candidate for renomination in 1882; elected to the Forty-ninth, Fiftieth, and Fifty-first Congresses (March 4, 1885-March 3, 1891); chairman, Committee on Private Land Claims (Fifty-first Congress); unsuccessful candidate for renomination in 1890; resumed the practice of law in Fort Atkinson, Jefferson County, Wis.; died in Fort Atkinson, Wis., April 26, 1919; interment in Evergreen Cemetery.

CATT, CARRIE CLINTON LANE CHAPMAN (1859-1947), was a suffragist and reformer, who played a major role in obtaining the vote for women.

Born in Ripon, Wisconsin on January 9, 1859, she attended Iowa State Agricultural College, receiving her B.S. degree in 1880 and graduating first in her class.

Her college education was hard to come by, as her father opposed her continuing her education. However she obtained a teaching certificate, taught school for a year, and earned enough money to begin college. She also supported herself by washing dishes and working in the library.

She intended to pursue law and began working for a lawyer, but was soon offered the position of principal at a nearby high school. Within two years, she was named superintendent of schools, a position unheard of for a woman during that time.

She remained superintendent until February of 1885 when she married Leo Chapman who owned the *Mason City Republican,* after which she began working as the newspaper's assistant editor. The couple decided they wanted to purchase another newspaper and Chapman traveled to California to check out a prospect, with his wife planning to follow him there later. However, before she was able to leave, Chapman fell ill with typhoid fever and died.

Once she reached California, she stayed for a year, working for a San Francisco newspaper. She then returned to Iowa and began giving lectures, and soon after, she became a member of the Iowa Woman Suffrage Association. When the National American Woman Suffrage Association was formed, she was an Iowa delegate to their first convention.

She remarried to civil engineer George William Catt who was extremely supportive of her feminist activities, even signing a contract which stated that she would be able to have two months in the spring and two months in the fall to pursue her suffrage work. The couple resided in Seattle for a time, then moved to New York City. Catt died in 1905, leaving his wife financially set, and she threw herself into her suffrage work full time.

However, before he died, he saw his wife become the new president of the National American Woman Suffrage Association, handpicked by incumbent president Susan B. Anthony who was getting on in years. When Carrie's husband became ill, she resigned her post in 1904 to Anna Howard Shaw, leaving a highly-organized, smooth-running, national women's organization.

After Mr. Catt's death, Carrie involved herself mainly with the New York, as well as the international branch of the movement. Later, she was once again called on to become president of the national organization, succeeding Anna Howard Shaw.

When she took over the reins of the National American Woman Suffrage Association, it was not the organization she had left, as there were now two different factions dividing it, with their main disagreement centering on how to attain the vote for women. While one side felt that the Democrats should be held accountable for their failure to pass the voting amendment, Catt was of the opinion that they should not lump the whole party together, therefore possibly alienating those Democrats who supported their cause. The leader of the opposing faction, Alice Paul resigned and Catt once again tried to bring a more cohesive spirit to the organization. She decided to approach the situation from a positive point of view and came up with what would later be dubbed the "Winning Plan," which entailed attaining the vote by concentrating not only on a federal amendment, but on the state legislatures as well as securing the right to vote in the primaries.

She was also insistent on keeping the women's issue alive during World War I, trying to prevent it from being put on the back burner. She teamed up with Jane Addams to form the Woman's Peace Party due to her pacifist leanings, but urged women to get involved in the war effort, feeling that if they showed their mettle in the nation's time of need, it might be impressive enough to help garner the right to vote.

Finally, after years of Catt's non-stop dedication to the cause, the federal amendment for the women's vote passed both the House and the Senate (fourteen months apart), with the final decision confirmed on August 26, 1920.

Catt worked tirelessly for the women's cause overseas, as well, involving herself with the International Woman Suffrage Alliance (which later became the International Alliance of Women), often presiding over its Congressional conferences in different countries such as London, Amsterdam, Berlin and Budapest. It was also her suggestion in 1919 to create a League of Women Voters, an organization that is still active today.

Catt was given numerous honors throughout her distinguished career, including several honorary degrees from various schools that included Iowa State College, Moravian College for Women and Smith College, as well as a citation of honor by President Roosevelt in 1936.

She was also the founder of the National Committee on the Cause and Cure of War, acting as its president from 1925 to 1932. After her death on March 9, 1947, at the age of eighty-eight, the League of Women Voters founded the Carrie Chapman Catt Memorial Foundation.

CLARK, CHARLES BENJAMIN, (1844-1881) a U. S. Representative from Wisconsin; born in Theresa, Jefferson County, N.Y., August 24, 1844; attended the common schools; moved to Wisconsin in 1855 with his widowed mother, who settled in Neenah, Winnebago County;

enlisted in Company I, Seventy-first Regiment, Wisconsin Volunteer Infantry, at its organization, and served with the same during the Civil War; engaged in mercantile pursuits, banking. and the manufacture of paper; mayor of Neenah 1880-1883; member of the city council of Neenah 1883-1885; member of the State assembly in 1885; elected as a Republican to the Fiftieth and Fifty-first Congresses (March 4, 1887-March 3, 1891); unsuccessful candidate for reelection in 1890 to the Fifty-second Congress; died in Watertown, Jefferson County, N.Y., while on a visit to his old home, September 10, 1881; interment in Oak Hill Cemetery, Neenah, Wis.

CLASSON, DAVID GUY, (1870-1923) a U. S. Representative from Wisconsin born in Oconto, Oconto County, Wis., September 27, 1870; attended the public schools, and was graduated from the law department of the University of Wisconsin at Madison in 1891; was admitted to the bar the same year and commenced practice in Oconto, Wis.; judge of Oconto County 1894-1898; mayor of Oconto 1898-1900; city attorney 1900-1906; president of the board of education in 1912 and 1913; president of the board of fire and police commissioners in 1915 and 1916; elected as a Republican to the Sixty-fifth, Sixty-sixth, and Sixty-seventh Congresses (March 4, 1917-March 3, 1923); declined to be a candidate for renomination in 1922; resumed the practice of law in Oconto, Wis.; served as circuit judge of the twentieth judicial circuit 1928-1930; died in Oconto, Wis., September 6, 1930; interment in Evergreen Cemetery.

COBURN, FRANK POTTER, (1858-1932) a U. S. Representative from Wisconsin; born on a farm near West Salem, La Crosse County, Wis., December 6, 1858; attended the public schools; engaged in agricultural pursuits near West Salem; also engaged in the banking business in West Salem; was an unsuccessful Democratic candidate for election in 1888 to the Fifty-Arst Congress; elected as a Democrat to the Fifty-second Congress (March 4, 1891-March 3, 1893); was an unsuccessful candidate for reelection in 1892 to the Fifty-third Congress; resumed banking interests and agricultural pursuits near West Salem, Wis.; member of the county board of supervisors 1894-1903, serving as chairman in 1902 and 1903; jury commissioner 1897-1932; trustee of the county asylum 1907-1932; member of the board of review of income taxes for the county 1912-1926; died in La Crosse, Wis., on November 2, 1932; interment in Hamilton Cemetery, West Salem, Wis.

COHEN, WILBUR JOSEPH (1913-1987), was an educator, author and Civil Servant.

Born in Milwaukee, Wisconsin on June 10, 1913, he attended the University of Wisconsin, receiving his Ph.B. degree in 1934.

Later that year, he began working as a research assistant in President Roosevelt's Cabinet Committee on Economic Security in Washington, D.C. The following year, he became a technical advisor at the U.S. Social Security Administration, a position he held until 1953, when he became director of Division of Research and Statistics for three years. In 1956, he worked as professor of public welfare administration at the University of Michigan in Ann Arbor, and in 1961 he moved back to Washington, D.C. to become the assistant secretary for legislation at the U.S. Department of Health, Education and Welfare. In 1965 he was promoted to undersecretary and in 1968, to secretary of the department. A year later he returned to the University of Michigan as professor of education and during that time also worked as dean of the School of Education. Ten years later he began working at the University of Texas at Austin, Lyndon B. Johnson School of Public Affairs becoming a professor in 1983.

He has been a member of the Advisory Council on Public Assistance, 1959; house of delegates, Council on Social Work Education, 1959-62, 1974-76; the National Committee on Social Security, 1978-81; the President's Committee on Mental Retardation, 1968; the President's Committee on Population and Family Planning, 1968; and the National Committee on Unemployment Compensation, 1978-80. He has been a United States respresentative at various international conferences regarding social work, social security, and labor, and has served as a consultant on aging to the U.S. Senate Committee on Labor and Public Welfare, 1956-57, 1959, and to the United Nations, 1956-57.

Cohen's other memberships include the American Economic Association, the American Public Welfare Association, the American Public Health Association, the National Association of Social Workers, and the Industrial Relations Research Association.

Cohen wrote several books, including: *Unemployment Insurance and Agricultural Labor in Great Britain*, 1940; *Retirement Policies under Social Security*, 1957;

and *Health in America: The Role of the Federal Government in Bringing High Quality Health Care to All American People*, 1968; among others.

Awards he was given include: the Distinguished Service Award, U.S. Department of Health, Education, and Welfare, and Group Health Association Award, both 1956; the Florina Lasker Award, National Conference on Social Welfare, and Terry Award, American Public Welfare Association, both 1961; awards from the National Association of Social Workers, the National Association for Mentally Retarded Children, and the Association of Physical Medicine, all 1965; and the Jane Addams-Hull House Award, 1975; among several others.

Cohen was married to Eloise Bittel and the couple had three sons. He died on May 17, 1987 in Seoul, South Korea.

COOK, SAMUEL ANDREW, (1849-1918) a U. S. Representative from Wisconsin; born in Ontario, Canada, January 28, 1849; moved with his parents to Calumet County, Wis., in 1856; attended the common schools in Fond do Lac and Calumet Counties; enlisted as a private in Company A, Second Wisconsin Cavalry, under General Caster, and served until the end of the Civil War; lived on a farm in Calumet County until 1872, when he located in Marathon County and engaged in business; moved to Neenah, Winnebago County, in 1881; elected mayor of Neenah in 1889; member of the State assembly in 1891 and 1892; delegate to the Republican National Convention at Minneapolis in 1892; elected as a Republican to the Fifty-fourth Congress (March 4, 1895-March 3, 1897); declined renomination in 1896; was an unsuccessful candidate for United States Senator in 1897 and again in 1907; commander of the Grand Army of the Republic for Department of Wisconsin in 1915 and 1916; became a manufacturer of paint paper at Menasha, Wis., with residence in Neenah, Wis.; president of the Alexandria Paper Company at Alexandria, Ind.; died in Neenah, Wis., on April 4, 1918; interment in Oak Hill Cemetery.

COOPER, HENRY ALLEN, (1851-1931) a U. S. Representative from Wisconsin; born in Spring Prairie, Walworth County, Wis., September 8, 1851; moved with his parents to Burlington, Wis., in 1851; attended the common schools; was graduated from Burlington High School in June 1869, from Northwestern University, Evanston, Ill., in 1873, and from Union College of Law (then the legal department of

31

Northwestern University and of the old University of
Chicago) in 1875; was admitted to the bar and commenced
practice at Burlington, Wis.; elected district attorney of
Racine County in November 1880; moved to the city of
Racine in January 1881; reelected district attorney without
opposition in 1882 and 1884; delegate to the Republican National Conventions in 1884, 1908, and 1924; member of the
State senate 1887-1889 and author of the bill which became
the law first establishing the Australian secret ballot
system in the State of Wisconsin; unsuccessful candidate
for election in 1890 to the Fifty-second Congress; elected as
a Republican to the Fifty-third and to the twelve succeeding
 Congresses (March 4, 1893-March 3, 1919); chairman,
Committee on Rivers and Harbors (Fifty-fifth Congress),
Committee on Insular Affairs (Fifty-sixth through Sixtieth
Congresses); unsuccessful candidate for reelection in 1918
to the Sixty-sixth Congress; again elected to the Sixty-
seventh and to the four succeeding Congresses and served
from March 4, 1921, until his death; had been reelected to
the Seventy-second Congress; died in Washington, D.C.

CORNELL, ROBERT JOHN, (December 16, 1919-) a U.
S. Representative from Wisconsin; born in Gladstone,
Delta County, Mich.; attended parochial schools in Green
Bay, Wis.; B.A., St. Norbert College, DePere, Wis., 1941;
M.A., Ph.D., Catholic University of America, Washington,
D.C., 1957; ordained a Roman Catholic priest, Norbertine
Order, 1944; teacher of social sciences in parochial schools
of Philadelphia, Pa., 1941-1947; professor of history and
political science, St. Norbert College, 1947-1974, and 1979 to
present; chairman, Eighth Congressional District
Democratic Party of Wisconsin, 1969-1974; member, State
Administrative Committee of Democratic Party of Wisconsin, 1969-1974; elected as a Democrat to the Ninety-fourth
and Ninety-fifth Congresses (January 3, 1975-January 3,
1979); unsuccessful candidate for reelection in 1978 to the
Ninety-sixth Congress; is a resident of DePere, Wis.

CROWLEY, LEO THOMAS (1889-1972), was an official
with the United States Government, as well as an
industrialist.
    Born in Milton Juncton, Wisconsin on August 15,
1889, he attended the University of Wisconsin.
    He became a businessman while in his late teens,
buying the grocery store where he had once worked as a
delivery boy. Soon after, he began working at the General
Paper and Supply Company, and at the age of twenty-one,

he was named president of the firm. He continued to hold, as he once wrote a friend, "a directorate now and then in insurance and banking, and, in Madison, Wisconsin, was president of St. Mary's Hospital."

Later on, when he was the president of the Bank of Wisconsin, he helped to support legislation that bolstered Wisconsin's banking system. During the Depression he founded the Wisconsin Banking Review Board which gave the State's banks a "firm foundation."

His star continued to rise when, in 1934, President Roosevelt requested that he be in charge of the newly created Federal Deposit Insurance Corporation, calling Crowley "a symbol of banking integrity." He also found himself in a rare, but lucrative situation when he was asked to become chairman of the board of the "billion dollar" Standard Gas and Electric Company, and he was able to accept with the blessing of President Roosevelt. In addition, according to *Time* Magazine, "with Mr. Roosevelt's apparent permission, he has assumed half a dozen directorates of other private companies."

In 1942, he was given another position of considerable responsibility when Roosevelt named him to head the Alien Property Office, a covert operation in which agents were to track down evidence of enemy control of American companies that had been seized by the Government for the duration of the War. Some of the companies his organization siezed included the Magnesium Development Corporation and Luscombe Airplane Corporation.

The following year, he gave up his profitable position with Standard Gas and Electric to become head of the Office of Economic Warfare, which had been experiencing some tumultuous infighting. When Crowley took the helm, he said his main objective was "to follow the foreign policy of the President and Secretary Hull."

In 1943, President Roosevelt decided to consolidate a group of government agencies such as the Office of Economic Warfare and the Office of Foreign Relief and Rehabilitation Operations, and merge them into one bureau, the Foreign Economic Administration. When Crowley was chosen to head this new organization, *Time* Magazine noted that he was "the czar of all foreign economic dealings, which are the guts of foreign relations." Roosevelt, himself, was effusive in his praise of Crowley's capabilities, saying, "Leo Crowley is one of the best administrators in or out of Government, and I find great satisfaction in promoting him to a position which will centralize all foreign economic operations in one operating agency."

Along with his governmental work, he was also heavily involved in the affairs of the Catholic Church and was decorated by Pope Pius XI with the St. Gregory, the great Order of Knight.

Crowley never married. He died on April 15, 1972.

CUSHING, WILLIAM BARKER (1842-1874), was a naval officer, known for his brave and adventurous feats during the Civil War.

Born in Delafield, Wisconsin on November 4, 1842, he studied for a short time at the Naval Academy.

Having lost his father at a young age, he helped support his mother by working as a page in the House of Representatives in 1856. He entered the Naval Academy a short time after, but had no patience with his studies and after he was caught playing a prank on one of his professors, he was asked to leave. However, when the Civil War began, he was able to attain the rank of acting master's mate on the ship *Minnesota*.

During the War, he proved himself to be an especially able sailor when he successfully brought captured prize ships into port on two occasions. He then formally entered the Navy at the rank of acting midshipman and was promoted to lieutenant before the age of twenty. By 1862, he was the executive officer of the *Commodore Perry* and when the ship ran aground, leaving it vulnerable for capture by the enemy, he saved it almost singlehandedly. As commander of the *Ellis*, he became legendary for his capture of various enemy ships, as well as the numerous raids he made on Confederate camps.

He continued to command other vessels such as the *Shokokon*, the *Commodore Barney* and the *Monticello*, while continuing his brave exploits. One of his most admired feats was his sinking of the last Confederate ironclad, the *Albemarle* which had a history of sinking many Union ships. During the battle, he and a crew member narrowly escaped death and got away by swimming down the river. The incident brought him a promotion to lieutenant commander and an expression of gratitude from Congress.

He continued taking over several enemy vessels, seemingly with great ease and his ability to survive his encounters without so much as a scratch brought him unwavering trust from his men and a proclamation from Secretary of the Navy Gideon Wells who called him "*the* hero of the war."

After being in charge of various squadrons, he was named ordnance officer of the Boston Navy Yard and two years later, in 1872, he was given the rank of commander, the youngest officer to hold that rank.

Unfortunately, his fearless exploits took their toll on him physically, and during a leave of absence from his command, he died of brain fever on December 17, 1874.

D

DALY, JAMES FIRMAN (1918-1978), was a stage, film and television actor.

Born in Wisconsin Rapids, Wisconsin on October 23, 1918, Daly attended three different colleges, the State University of Iowa, the University of Wisconsin, and Cornell College, receiving a B.A. degree from the latter in 1941.

Soon after his graduation, he enlisted in the United States Army and was then transferred to the Army Air Forces.

After leaving the service, Daly pursued his acting career in earnest, and secured a part as the understudy for actor Gary Merrill in the Broadway comedy hit *Born Yesterday*.

He continued doing stage work such as *Virginia Reel*, Bernard Shaw's *Man and Superman* and Shelley's *The Cenci*. For his work in the last role, a reviewer wrote, "James Daley proves that he rates with any classical actor alive today." He was then involved in two more of Shaw's plays, as understudy in *The Devil's Disciple* and as Bill Walker in *Major Barbara*, winning a Theatre World Award for the latter. His other plays during that period were *Billy Budd*, *Mary Rose* and *Saint Joan*.

Daly began his television work in 1953, landing the starring role in the series *Foreign Intrigue*. While filming the show in Europe, he also appeared on the *Omnibus* series, doing roles in such works as *Henry Adams*, *The Court Martial of William Mitchell* and *Lee at Gettysburg*. After his return to the States, he appeared on the *Kraft Television Theater* and *Studio One*, and was also a long-time spokesman for Camel cigarettes.

His first role on screen was the film version of *The Court Martial of Billy Mitchell*, in 1955. Other films of his include *The Young Stranger*, 1957; *Planet of the Apes*, 1968; *The Big Bounce*, 1968; *Wild in the Sky*, 1972; and *The Resurrection of Zachary Wheeler*, 1973.

He continued his stage work in such plays as *Miss Julie*, 1956; *The Glass Menagerie*, 1956; *Back to Methuselah*, 1958; *J.B.*, 1959; *Period of Adjustment*,

1960; *Who's Afraid of Virginia Woolf?*, 1965; and *A Moon for the Misbegotten*, 1965.

Daly is perhaps best known for his television role opposite Chad Everett on the series *Medical Center* which ran from 1969 to 1975.

Daly was married to Mary Hope Newell and the couple had four children, including actors Tyne Daly and Timothy Daly. He died in 1978.

DAVIDSON, JAMES HENRY, (1859-1918) a U. S. Representative from Wisconsin; born in Colchester, Delaware County, N.Y., June 18, 1858; attended the public schools and Walton (N.Y.) Academy; taught school in Delaware and Sullivan Counties, N.Y.; was graduated from the Albany Law School in 1884 and was admitted to the bar the same year; moved to Green Lake County, Wis., and commenced practice in Princeton in 1887; also taught school; elected district attorney of Green Lake County in 1888; chairman of the Republican congressional committee for the sixth district of Wisconsin in 1890; moved to Oshkosh, Wis., January 1, 1892, and continued the practice of law; appointed city attorney in May 1895 for two years; elected as a Republican to the Fifty-fifth and to the seven succeeding Congresses (March 4, 1897-March 3, 1913); chairman, Committee on Railways and Canals (Fifty-sixth through Sixty-first Congresses); unsuccessful candidate for reelection in 1912 to the Sixty-third Congress and for election in 1914 to the Sixty-fourth Congress; resumed the practice of his profession; elected to the Sixty-fifth Congress and served from March 4, 1917, until his death in Washington, D.C., August 6, 1918; interment in Riverside Cemetery, Oshkosh, Wis.

DAVIES, JOSEPH EDWARD (1876-1958), was a lawyer, a diplomat, and an author.

Born in Watertown, Wisconsin on November 29, 1876, he received an A.B. degree from the University of Wisconsin in 1898 and an LL.B degree in 1901.

After passing the Bar in 1901, he practiced law in his home state until 1913, during which he was State's attorney for four years. He then went to Washington, D.C. and worked in various legal capacities for the government, becoming the economic advisor to President Wilson at the Versailles Conference in 1918. In 1920, he was counsel for the government of Mexico, then continued in this vein for various other countries, including Peru, Holland, Greece, and the Dominican Republic, as well as the United States.

From 1924 to 1927, he was counsel for the U.S. taxpayers in the Ford Stock Valuation Tax Case and from 1932 to 1936 he was counsel to the President of the Republic of Santo Domingo in refinancing an external loan.

After serving as the U.S. ambassador to Russia from 1936 to 1938, and to Belgium in 1938-39, he returned to private practice in 1941. However, he once again became involved in government affairs two years later when President Roosevelt asked him to act as special envoy (with the rank of ambassador), to confer with Marshal Stalin from May to June of 1943. He was given the same rank by President Truman for a conference with Prime Minister Winston Churchill in June of 1945, as well as for the important Potsdam Conference in July and August.

Other special appointments he was given include: special assistant to Secretary of State Hull, in charge of War Emergency Problems and Policies, 1939-41; vice chairman Democratic National Commission, 1936; chairman of President Roosevelt's Inaugural Commission, 1941 and 1945; and chairman of the President's War Relief Control Board, 1942-46.

Davies was given several honors during his long and distinguished career including the Medal for Merit (highest civilian decoration of U.S.), 1946 and decorations from numerous countries such as France, Peru, Greece, Russia, Belgium, Santo Domingo and Panama, among others.

Davies also contributed articles to various periodicals and wrote major reports on such issues as Farm Machinery, Fertilizer, Oil, Lumber and Taxation of Corporations. He was author of the book, *Mission to Moscow*.

Joseph Davies died on May 9, 1958.

DERLETH, AUGUST WILLIAM (1909-1971), was an author of novels and poems.

Born in Sauk City, Wisconsin on February 24, 1909, he received a B.A. degree from the University of Wisconsin in 1930.

He began his career as an associate editor at Fawcett Publications in 1930, staying a year before going out on his own as a freelance writer. In 1939, he became publisher of Arkham House in his home town of Sauk City and beginning in 1941, also worked as literary editor of *The Capital Times* in Madison. Derleth had his own weekly column and was an occasional lecturer at the University of Wisconsin.

His novels included: *Still is the Summer Night*, 1937; *Wind Over Wisconsin*, 1938; *Restless is the River*, 1939; *Evening in Spring*, 1941; *Sweet Genevieve*, 1942; *Shadow of Night*, 1943; and *The Shield of the Valiant*, 1945.

He also wrote shorter works of fiction, such as: *Place of Hawks*, 1935; *Country Growth*, 1940; *Sac Prairie People*, 1948; *The House of Moonlight*, 1963; and *Wisconsin in Their Bones*, 1961.

His published poetry includes: *Hawk on the Wind*, 1938; *Man Track Here*, 1939; *Here on a Darkling Plain*, 1940; *Wind in the Elms*, 1941; *Selected Poems*, 1944; *The Edge of Night*, 1945; *Rendezvous in a Landscape*, 1952; *West of Morning*, 1960; and *The Only Place We Live* ; among others.

Derleth was an extremely prolific writer who wrote historical books, biographies, children's books and supernatural fiction, as well as numerous articles for over five hundred magazines and newspapers such as *Nature*, *Saturday Review*, *New Republic*, *Atlantic Monthly*, *Country Gentlemen*, and *New Yorker*.

He once said of his work: "I believe that all writing-- all creative art--is a way of communicating with one's fellowmen and with one's self. I have nothing to say that has not been said before, but much of what has been said before is worth repeating, and what I say in such books as *Walden West* and *Evening in Spring*, *Village Year*, *Country Growth*, *The Shield of the Valiant*, remains true from one generation to another."

August Derleth was married to Sandra Evelyn (later divorced) and the couple had two children. He died on July 4, 1971.

DEUSTER, PETER VICTOR, (1831-1904) a U. S. Representative from Wisconsin; born near Aix to Chapelle, Rhenish Prussia, February 13, 1831; pursued an academic course; immigrated to the United States with his parents, who settled on a farm near Milwaukee, Wis., in May 1847; worked in a printing office; moved to Port Washington, Wis., in 1854 and edited a newspaper; also served simultaneously as postmaster, clerk of the circuit court, clerk of the land office, and notary public; returned to Milwaukee in 1856 and edited the Milwaukee See-Bote, a Democratic daily paper, until 1860, when he became proprietor; member of the State assembly in 1863; served in the State senate in 1870 and 1871; elected as a Democrat to the Forty-sixth, Forty-seventh, and Forty-eighth Congresses (March 4, 1879-March 3, 1885); chairman, Committee on Expenditures on Public Buildings (Forty-sixth Congress); unsuccessful candidate for reelection in 1884 to the Forty-ninth Congress; resumed newspaper interests; appointed chairman of a commission to diminish the Umatilla Indian Reservation in Oregon in 1887; appointed consul at Crefeld, Germany, February 19, 1896, and served until a successor was appointed October 15, 1897; died in Milwaukee, Wis., December 31, 1904; interment in Calvary Cemetery.

DEWEY, NELSON (1813-1889), first state governor of Wisconsin (1848-52), was born in Lebanon, Connecticut, December 19, 1813, son of Ebenezer and Lucy (Webster) Dewey. In 1814 his family moved to Butternuts, New York, and in 1829 he was sent to be educated at the academy in Hamilton, New York. After remaining there for three years, he taught school for a year in Morris, New York. Upon moving to Lancaster, Wisconsin in 1836, he began to study law and was admitted to the bar two years later. Dewey assisted in organizing Grant County in 1837, was elected its first registrar of deeds, and represented it in the territorial legislative assembly during 1838-42, serving as speaker at the extra session of that body in August, 1840. A member of the territorial council, 1842-46, he acted as president of that body during its fourth session in January of the latter year.

On the admission of Wisconsin to the Union on May 29, 1848, Dewey was elected its first state governor, and was re-elected in 1850, serving from June 7, 1848 until January 5, 1852. In 1854-55 he was state senator and for a number of years one of the commissioners of the state prison. After that he held no public offices except those of delegate to nearly every Democratic state convention, and presidential elector in 1888.

As governor, in the trying period of the first years of the state's existence, Dewey's conduct of affairs proved advantageous to the commonwealth, and many of the business methods orginated by him are still practiced in parts of the state. Governor Dewey was elected president of the Wisconsin Historical Society in 1849, and he was one of the pioneers in developing the lead mining industry in the state. He was married during his first term as governor, to Kate, daughter of Charles Dunn, the territorial chief justice of Wisconsin. He died in Cassville, Wisconsin, July 21, 1889.

DIETRICH, NOAH (1889-1982), was a financial advisor whose most famous client was Howard Hughes.
Born in Batavia, Wisconsin on February 28, 1889,

Dietrich's first job was as a bank teller in Maxwell, New Mexico during 1910-1911. From 1911 to 1917, he worked as an auditor at Los Angeles Suburban Land Co., then moved to New York to work as assistant comptroller at E.L. Doheny for three years. In 1920, he returned to Los Angeles and joined Haskins & Sells as a senior accountant. He had a four year position with H.L. Arnold before becoming executive assistant to Howard Hughes at the latter's company, Hughes Tool Co. in 1925. He worked in that capacity for twenty years, becoming executive vice president in 1945 and corporate consultant in 1957.

During the time he was associated with Hughes' corporation, he also held various other positions such as: commissioner with the city of Los Angeles from 1955 to 1971; director and regional vice-president of the National Association of Manufacturers, 1941-1950; chairman of RKO, 1949-1955; director and chairman of the finance committee of Trans-World Airlines; director of Gulf Brewing Co. and director of National Bank of Commerce in Houston.

He was a member of the original board of regents of the University of Houston and was a delegate to President Harry S. Truman's post-World War II Labor-Management Conference.

In 1957, Dietrich was fired by Howard Hughes after an acrimonious dispute over financial matters. He retaliated years later by writing the biography *Howard: The Amazing Mr. Hughes* in which he made controversial accusations concerning Hughes' sanity.

Dietrich was married three times and had five children. He died in Palm Springs, California on February 15, 1982.

DILWEG, LAVERN RALPH, (November 1, 1903-January 2, 1968) a U. S. Representative from Wisconsin; born in Milwaukee, Wis.; attended the public schools; was graduated from the law department of Marquette University, Milwaukee, Wis., in 1927; was admitted to the bar in 1927 and commenced practice in Green Bay, Wis.; played professional football 1926-1934 and continued his connection with the game as an official in the Big Ten until 1943; connected with construction work and a number of business concerns in Green Bay, Wis.; in charge of Home Owners Loan Corporation, Green Bay, Wis., area 1934-1942; elected as a Democrat to the Seventy-Eighth Congress (January 3,1943 January 3, 1945); unsuccessful candidate for reelection in 1944 to the Seventy-ninth Congress; resumed the

DIXON, JEANE L.

practice of law in Green Bay, Wis., and Washington, D.C.;
confirmed as a member of the Foreign Claims Settlement
Commission April 13, 1961; died in St. Petersburg, Fla.;
interment in Fort Howard Ceme cemetary, Green Bay, Wis.

DIXON, JEANE L. (ne Pinckert), (1918-) is a well-known
psychic who's most famous prediction was the assassination of President John F. Kennedy.

She was born in Medford, Wisconsin and raised in a
family of six children, who all spoke German as their first
language. When she was still a child, her family moved
to Santa Rosa, California, and she began to show her
psychic abilities even then. At the age of eight, her mother
took her to a gypsy woman who noticed the unique lines on
the palms of her hands--a large star on her right hand and
the star of David on her left. She was given a crystal ball
by the gypsy and her mother was told that Jeane had the
gift of prophecy.

Dixon attended high school in Los Angeles and was involved in numerous activities including singing and acting, at one time appearing as Mary Magdalene in *The
Life of Christ*, a play staged at the Hollywood Bowl.

After marrying James L. Dixon at the age of twenty-
one, the couple eventually moved to Detroit and after
World War II began, they moved to Washington, D.C.
where he was in charge of real estate acquisitions for
warehouses and depots.

It was in Washington that Dixon began doing
readings, initially as entertainment for the GI's at parties
sponsored by a women's group, the Home Hospitality Committee. Her reputation for accurate readings soon spread
into the upper echelon of Washington and she began
reading for various political figures and dignitaries.

When the war was over, her husband James began
his own real estate business and Jeane began working
side-by-side with him in the venture. She continued to
make a name for herself in Washington with her predictions, forecasting such events as the partition of India, the
communist takeover of China and the murder of Mahat-
ma Gandhi. However it was her prediction of President
John F. Kennedy's assassination that made her a national figure. Thirteen years prior, she had given an interview to *Parade* magazine in which she stated that "a
Democratic President, elected in 1960--a tall young man
with blue eyes and thick brown hair--would die in office," a
vision she had in 1952 while she was praying.

Her vision was even clearer as November 22, 1963

42

approached and she supposedly tried to warn Kennedy to stay home and not make the trip to Dallas, her prediction being that he would be killed in the South by a person whose name began with O or Q.

After her prophecy turned out to be right, she had a book written about her psychic gifts by newspaper writer Ruth Montgomery entitled *A Gift of Prophecy: the Phenomenal Jeane Dixon* which sold almost three million in hardcover and millions more in paperback. Dixon began to get thousands of requests for readings and also became a popular speaker on the lecture circuit. She later wrote her own books such as *My Life and Prophecies*, 1969, *Reincarnation and Prayers to Live By*, 1970, *The Call to Glory*, 1972, *Yesterday, Today and Forever*, 1976, and *Horoscopes for Dogs (Pets and Their Planets)*, 1979. She has also had her own syndicated column *Horoscope and Predictions*. While a number of her predictions have not panned out, another major vision was that Robert Kennedy would be assassinated in California.

She is the founder of the Children-to-Children Foundation and has received numerous awards for her charity work.

DOLLARD, JOHN (1900-1980), was a social psychologist, educator and author.

Born in Menasha, Wisconsin on August 29, 1900, he wrote the controversial book *Caste and Class in a Southern Town* (1937) which concerned black repression, and was banned in Georgia.

His other books include *Social Learning and Imitation*, 1941; *Personality and Psychotherapy*, 1950 (both with N.E. Miller); *Scorning Human Motives*, 1959 (with Frank Auld, Jr.) and *Children of Bondage*, 1964.

Dollard was a professor of psychology at Yale University for seventeen years. He died on October 8, 1980.

DREYFUS, LEE SHERMAN (1926-), Wisconsin's thirty-ninth governor, was born in Milwaukee on June 20, 1926, the son of Woods Orlow and Clare (Bluett) Dreyfus. He attended the University of Wisconsin, and graduated in 1957 with a Ph.D in communications. During World War II, he served in the U.S. Navy as an electronic technician. In 1947, Dreyfus married Joyce Mae Unke. They had two children.

While still at the university, Dreyfus began work as a radio actor for station WISN in Milwaukee. He was an instuctor at the University of Wisconsin for three years. Over the suceeding ten years, he had various positions: general manager of radio station WDET in Detroit; assistant professor, associate professor of Speech, and associate director of Mass Communications at Wayne State University. From 1962-65, he was general manager for WHA television in Madison. He was professor of Speech, and Chairman of the Radio-TV and Films Division at the University of Wisconsin-Madison from 1962 to 1967. He also served as Director of Instructional Resources. From 1967 to 1969, he was president (later called chancellor) of Wisconsin State University at Stevens Point.

Dreyfus entered politics in 1978 as the Republican candidate for governor. His prominence in education and media around the state had allowed him to cultivate many friends, and although he ran a grass-roots campaign, he won over Martin Schreiber by a vote of 816,056 to 673,813. His effectiveness in communicating via the media gained him popularity. As governor, Dreyfus was faced with an opposition legislature, which attempted to block many of his programs. He was successful in reducing income taxes and deregulating the trucking industry. He created the Department of Development, supported tough sentencing for criminals, and signed into law a bill to prohibit discrimination because of sexual preference. Later in his term he attempted to diminish the soaring state deficit through reduced state spending, a five-cent per gallon gasoline tax, and an increase in state sales tax. He declined to seek reelection in 1982. Following his term in office, Dreyfus went to work as president of Sentry Insurance.

DUFFY, FRANCIS BRAN, (1888-1979) a U. S. Senator from Wisconsin; born in Fond do Lac, Fond do Lac County, Wis., June 23, 1888; attended the public schools; was graduated from the University of Wisconsin at Madison, in 1910 and from its law department in 1912; was admitted to the bar in 1912 and commenced practice in Fond do Lac, Wis.; during the First World War served in the United States Army 1917-1919, attaining the rank of major; resumed the practice of law in Fond do Lac, Wis.; elected as a Democrat to the United States Senate and served from March 4, 1933, to January 3, 1939; unsuccessful candidate for reelection in 1938; again resumed the practice of law before becoming United States district judge for the eastern district of Wisconsin, serving from 1939 to 1949, when he qualified as a United States circuit judge of the court of appeals for the seventh circuit, becoming chief judge in 1954 and served until 1959; retired as a full-time member of the court in 1966 and assumed the status of senior judge and continued to hear cases for several more years; died in Milwaukee, Wis., August 16, 1979; interment in Calvary Cemetery, Fond do Lac, Wis.

E

EARL, ANTHONY S. (April 12, 1936-), Wisconsin's for-
tieth governor, was born in Michigan. He attended
Michigan State University at East Lansing where he
received a bachelor's degree in political science in 1958. In
1961 he graduated from the University of Chicago Law
School and passed the bar in both Wisconsin and Minnesota. From 1962 to 1965, Earl served in the U.S. Navy.
He married Sheila Coyle of Chicago in 1962. They had four
daughters.

In 1965, Earl was appointed Assistant District Attorney of Marathon County, Wisconsin. He served for a
year, then became the first full-time City Attorney of
Wausau. In 1969, he ran for State Assembly and won, serving the remainder of a term left open by the departure of
David Obey. He was reelected to a full term in 1970 and was
named to the Joint Committee on Finance. In 1971, his col-
leagues selected him to serve as majority leader. He held
that position until he left the legislature in January, 1975.
Earl ran for state attorney general in 1974, but was
defeated. Later that year, Governor Lucey appointed him
Secretary of the Department of Administration, a cabinet
position. The following year, he became Secretary of the
Department of Natural Resources.

Earl served as Wisconsin's chief environmental officer from December, 1975 until 1980, when he returned to
private law practice as a partner in the firm of Foley and
Lardner. He ran for governor in 1982, and defeated
Republican Terry Kohler by a margin of 57 percent to 42
percent. He was inaugurated on January 3, 1983. In addition
to his work as governor, Earl held various national posts
including that of chairman of the National Governors
Association's Standing Committee on Energy and the En-
vironment. He also was a member of the Democratic National Committee's Fairness Commission and Policy Commission. He was chair of the Council of Great Lakes Governors from 1983-85. Earl completed his term as governor in
January, 1987.

F

FARWELL, LEONARD (1819-1889), second governor of
Wisconsin (1852-54), was born in Watertown, New York,
January 5, 1819, son of Captain James and Rebecca (Cady)
Farwell. His mother died in 1824, and his father in 1830.
After a short experience as clerk in a dry-goods store, he
became apprentice to a tinsmith, and followed that occupation until the age of nineteen. He then established
himself in the hardware business at Lockport, Illinois,
and in 1840 moved to Milwaukee, where he soon had one of
the largest wholesale houses in the West. Ten years later
Farwell withdrew from business to engage in other enterprises. In 1847 he made a large purchase of real estate in
the city of Madison, where he took up residence and began
improvements on a large scale.

Farwell was a non-partisan anti-slavery Whig and,
although strongly averse to politics, was induced to accept the Whig nomination for governor of Wisconsin in
1851. Warmly supported by the Free Soilers and Aboli-
tionists, he defeated his Democratic opponent D. A. J.
Upham, by a narrow margin, the remainder of the state
ticket being Democratic. Farwell filled the gubernatorial
chair from 1852 until Janaury 2, 1854. During his administration an attempt was made to impeach Levi Hub-
bell, judge of the Milwaukee circuit, which was the first
and only instance of the impeachment of a judicial officer
in Wisconsin. In 1853 an act was passed abolishing capital
punishment for murder and substituting imprisonment
for life at hard labor. Wisconsin was the first state to
abolish the gallows, and this startling innovation in the
history of jurisprudence was mainly due to the efforts of
Marvin H. Bovee, then a member of the senate of Wisconsin. Another important act provided for a geological survey
of the state, the governor appointing Edward Daniels first
state geologist. The same year the question of passing a
prohibitory liquor law was passed.

After retiring from office, Governor Farwell
resumed his business affairs and became largely interested in railroad enterprises, but failed during the

financial revulsion of 1857. In the spring of 1863 President Lincoln appointed him assistant examiner in the patent office in Washington. He was promoted to the office of principal examiner of inventions three months later, a position he held for seven years. Farwell then resigned to re-embark in business at Chicago, but lost much of his property in the great fire in October, 1871. Subsequently, he went to Grant City, Missouri, where he spent the remainder of his life. He was married September 20, 1853, to Frances A. Cross. She died in Washington, D.C., April 15, 1868. Governor Farwell died in Grant City, Missouri, April 10, 1889.

FERBER, EDNA-(1887-1968), author, was born in Kalamazoo, Michigan, August 15, 1887, daughter of Jacob Charles and Julia (Neuman) Ferber. Her father was a Jewish immigrant from Hungary. She received a public school education and, on graduation from high school, secured her first job as a reporter on the *Daily Courant* of Appleton, Wisconsin. She wrote for the Milwaukee *Journal* for four years, and then worked on the Chicago *Tribune*. She took up magazine work in 1911 following the publication of her first short story "The Homely Heroine" in *Everybody's* and of her first book *Dawn O'Hara* (1911).

Edna Ferber remained a prolific producer of magazine fiction about intimacy with the family, neighborhood life in small towns, and a variety of working women. Her short stories became popular through the magazines of large circulation, including the *Saturday Evening Post, Cosmopolitan, Women's Home Journal*, and the *Butterick* publications. Most of them were collected in book form under the titles of *Buttered Side Down* (1912), *Roast Beef Medium* (1913), *Personality Plus* (1914), *Emma McChesney & Co.* (1915), *Fanny Herself* (1917), *Cheerful—by Request* (1922), and *Mother Knows Best* (1927). Her novels include *The Girls* (1921), *So Big* (1924), *Show Boat* (1926), *Cimarron* (1930), *Giant* (1954) and *Ice Palace* (1958).

Ms. Ferber was also co-author with George V. Hobart of the comedy, *Our Mrs. Chesney*, in which Ethel Barrymore starred with George S. Kaufman. A number of her short stories were graded as the best of their year of publication by Edward J. O'Brien, and one, "Half Portions," won the O. Henry Memorial Prize for 1919.

In bulk her copious short-story production was rated as revealing an unmatched skill in efficient structure and style according to magazine standards and, though rarely transcending that form of fiction, never fell below it. She reproduced with illuminating flashes certain strata of American life, especially in cities, which she knew well. Her settings in this milieu were chiefly peopled with dynamic female characters, flappers and debutantes, chambermaids and actresses, shop girls and stenographers. In lively, crisp narration she told how they dressed and talked and of their working philosophy. In her novels Miss Ferber took a skillful grasp of community and family life from generation to generation, and viewed her terrain with a fine command of perspective and detail. Her retrospective and panoramic treatment of time and locale was seen in *Show Boat* and *Cimarron*, the former in picturing frontier life on the Mississippi, and the latter in its setting against the spectacular settlement of Oklahoma in 1889.

Edna Ferber died in 1968.

FREAR, JAMES ARCHIBALD, (1861-1939) a U. S. Representative from Wisconsin; born in Hudson, St. Croix County, Wis., October 24, 1861; attended the public schools, and Laurence University, Appleton, Wis., in 1878; moved with his parents to Washington, D.C., in 1879; served in the Signal Service, United States Army, 1879-1884; was graduated from the National Law University, Washington, D.C., in 1884; was admitted to the bar the same year and commenced practice in Hudson, Wis.; city attorney of Hudson in 1894 and 1895; served eleven years with the Wisconsin National Guard, retiring with the rank of colonel and judge advocate; district attorney of St. Croix County 1896-1901; member of the State assembly in 1903; served in the State senate in 1905; secretary of state of Wisconsin 1907-1913; elected as a Republican to the Sixty-third and to the ten succeeding Congresses (March 4, 1913-January 3, 1935); was not a candidate for renomination in 1934; resumed the practice of law in Washington, D.C., where he died May 28, 1939; interment in Arlington National Cemetery.

G

GALE, ZONA (1874-1938), was an author who wrote novels, poetry and short stories.

Born in Portage, Wisconsin, she attended the University of Wisconsin, receiving an M.A. degree in 1899. She began her career as a newspaper reporter for the *Evening Wisconsin*, later switching to the *Milwaukee Journal*. She moved to New York in 1901 and got a job working for the *Evening World*.

While working as a reporter, she wrote poetry and romantic fiction, although all of it was unpublished at the time. In 1903, she decided to quit her newspaper job and concentrate on her freelance writing. Some of the first stories she had published concerned an elderly couple which she entitled *The Loves of Pelleas and Etarre*.

A visit back home to Portage stirred her into writing about small town pleasures and she compiled a group of stories that eventually became several volumes, the first called *Friendship Village*, which was serialized in magazines including *Woman's Home Companion*, and *Atlantic*. After moving back to Portage for good, she continued her series, publishing *Mothers to Men*, 1911, *When I Was a Little Girl*, 1913, and *Neighborhood Stories*, 1914.

As she got older, she became an unwavering pacifist and wrote an anti-war book entitled *Heart's Kindred*. She also became heavily involved in women's suffrage, becoming a member of the Women's Trade Union league, the General Federation of Women's Clubs and the Wisconsin Woman Suffrage Association. Due to her involvement in these various causes, the tone of her novels changed, as in *A Daughter of the Morning* (1917), which exposed small-town limitations, especially where women were concerned.

In 1918, she wrote a tome entitled *Birth* in which the main character, a man, is misunderstood by the residents of a small town, and his death gives his son the freedom to make a new life elsewhere. The book was later dramatized as *Mister Pitt* in 1924. Her next book, *Miss Lulu Bett* also about a small town, had a lighter tone to it and became her most famous work. She also wrote a stage dramatization for it and in 1921 she received the Pulitzer Prize for drama.

She continued to be prolific in her later years, writing such books as *Faint Perfume*, 1923; *Preface to a Life*, 1926; *Yellow Gentians and Blue*, 1927; *Portage, Wisconsin*, 1929; *Old Fashioned Tales*, 1933; *Papa LaFleur*, 1933; *Light Woman*, 1937; and *Magna*, 1937.

In 1928, at the age of fifty-three, she married a businessman, William Llywelyn Breese, whom she had known since childhood. She had previously adopted one child, and also took in his adopted daughter as well.

Zona Gale died on December 27, 1938.

GARLAND, (HANNIBAL) HAMLIN (1860-1940), was a novelist and short story author whose writing style was self-described as "veritism."

Born in West Salem, Wisconsin on September 4, 1860, his family moved to Iowa when Garland was nine. In his early twenties he left home and traveled back to Wisconsin in order to find work. In 1883, he went to South Dakota and staked a claim to a piece of land, later selling it for $200. He then moved to Boston and tried unsuccessfully to get into Harvard. Deciding to pursue education on his own, he spent numerous hours in the Boston Public Library reading the works of Huxley, Haeckel, Helmholtz and Darwin, among others.

In 1884, he entered the Boston School of Oratory and later became a teacher there. During this time, he met some of the most prominent scholars of the day including Oliver Wendell Holmes, Edward Everett Hale, Edwin Booth, Minot Savage and William Dean Howells. It was through these people that he began to receive invitations to lecture before various groups.

After a visit home to see his family where he got an eye-opening view of the harsh life of the Midwestern farmer, he returned to Boston and proceeded to write several stories on the subject that were compiled into the book *Main-Travelled Roads* (1891). His other compilations included *Prairie Folk*, 1892, and *Wayside Courtships*, 1897.

Garland tried to convey the need for social and economic reforms in his work and he continued in that vein in his novels *A Member of the Third House*, *Jason Edwards* and *A Spoil of Office*, and the shorter work *A Little Norsk*. He also published a collection of essays entitled *Crumbling Idols* and the novel *Rose of Dutcher's Coolly* (1895).

Although the latter book was thought to be his best work, it was not a best-seller. Tired of writing about social reform, he wrote several novels about the romance and color of the Western frontier, books that were considered inferior to his other works, but that were extremely popular with his readers. This group of books included *The Captain of the Gray Horse Troop* (1902), which was ahead of its time due to its inference to the sometimes inhuman treatment of Indians; *Hesper*, 1903; *Money Magic*, 1907; *Cavanaugh, Forest Ranger*, 1910; and *Forester's Daughter*, 1914.

In 1917 he published what was considered to be his autobiography entitled *A Son of the Middle Border*, a book he had actually started around 1898. His other books during that period were *A Daughter of the Middle Border*, 1921, which was awarded the Pulitzer Prize, *Trail-Makers of the Middle Border*, 1926, and *Back-Trailers from the Middle Border*, 1928. Someone was quoted as saying that this group of books "form an epic of migration, of struggle and discouragement, of the conquest of unfriendly nature, and of human indifference which no historian of literature or of life may neglect."

Around 1930, Garland moved to California and continued to write such books as *Roadside Meetings*, 1930; *Companions on the Trail*, 1931; *My Friendly Contemporaries*, 1932; *Afternoon Neighbors*, 1934; as well as two books touching on his belief in spiritualism, *Forty Years of Psychic Research*, 1936, and *The Mystery of the Buried Crosses*, 1939.

Described as one of the "chief forerunners of American realism," he concurred, once saying that "Truth is a higher quality than beauty."

Hamlin Garland died on March 4, 1940.

GASSER, HERBERT SPENCER (1888-1963), was a physiologist and one-time director of the Rockefeller Institute for Medical Research.

Born in Platteville, Wisconsin on July 5, 1888, he attended the University of Wisconsin, receiving an A.B. degree in 1910, an A.M. degree in 1911 and in 1915, he was awarded an M.D. degree from Johns Hopkins.

After receiving his Master's degree, he began studying with a well-respected pharmacologist, A.S. Loevenhart who was able to discern Gasser's abilities immediately and called him his "scientific heir." During this period, Gasser worked as an assistant instructor in physiology.

In 1916, Gasser taught pharmacology at the University of Wisconsin and the following year he moved to St. Louis, Missouri to attend Washington University, where he worked under Joseph Erlanger.

During World War I, Gasser was a pharmacologist in the research division of the Chemical Warfare Service at the American University Experimental Station in Washington, D.C. He was also involved in research regarding the cause and treatment of traumatic shock.

After the war, he returned to Washington University as an associate physiology instructor and two years later he was promoted to associate professor. Gasser became head of the pharmacology department in 1921; however, he asked for a two-year leave of absence in order to travel to Europe and pursue his studies.

In 1919, he began research with Dr. H. Sidney Newcomer, and later worked with Joseph Erlanger, in what would become a major breakthrough concerning muscle-nerve physiology. The technique was described in Newsweek: "Mystery cloaks the process by which primary sense organs react upon nerve fibers and flash impulses to the brain. What goes on in a stimulated nerve? Why do some fibers communicate only cold, others heat, others pain? How do we become aware of sensations? These problems, keys to the mechanism of thought, would remain scientific blinds spots. But Dr. Gasser perfected an apparatus (the cathode ray oscillograph) delicate enough to register the infinitesimal electric currents set up by the stimulated nerve...From radio, just out of its infancy, he borrowed a new technique. He got the required voltage with a vacuum tube that amplified the nerve current...Upon a photographic screen the beam flashed a precise picture of nerve reaction."

After his breakthrough work, Gasser was offered a full professorship in physiology at Cornell Medical College in 1931, a position he stayed in for four years. He was then offered the prestigious post of director of the Rockefeller Institute for Medical Research. *Newsweek*, commenting on the appointment said: "At his hand lie inestimable opportunities to improve mankind's condition."

In 1944, Gasser and Erlanger were jointly awarded the Nobel Prize in Physiology and Medicine. Gasser made the decision to put his share of the money back into research, saying "That was the spirit in which the money was given, and I think it would be a good way in which to spend it."

One of his professors had described Gasser's devotion to his research years before, saying: "At no time has Dr. Gasser ever divorced himself for one instant from his laboratory researches. They began in his student days and have constantly increased in significance, volume, and importance..."

Gasser died in May of 1963.

GAULT, WILLIAM CAMPBELL

GAULT, WILLIAM CAMPBELL (1910-?), is a writer of
mystery novels and juvenile fiction who occasionally uses
the pseudonyms Will Duke and Roney Scott.

Born in Milwaukee, Wisconsin on March 9, 1910, he attended the University of Wisconsin in 1929.

Gault has always been a freelance writer, and in the
lean times, has supported himself by various odd jobs such
as hotel manager, waiter, busboy, mailman and shoe sole
cutter. He also worked for a time as secretary for the
Channel Cities Funeral Society.

His first mystery, published in 1952, was entitled
Don't Cry for Me. Some of his other mysteries include:
The Canvas Coffin, 1953; *Run, Killer, Run*, 1954; *Ring
Around Rosa*, 1955; *Square in the Middle*, 1956; *The Con-
vertible Hearse*, 1957; *Night Lady*, 1958; *Sweet Wild
Wench*, 1959; *Come Die with Me*, 1959; *County Kill*, 1962;
and *The Dead Seed*, 1985.

A partial list of his juvenile works include: *Thunder
Road*, 1952; *Mr. Quarterback*, 1955; *Rough Road to Glory*,
1958; *Two Wheeled Thunder*, 1962; *The Oval Playground*,
1968; *Gasoline Cowboy*, 1974; *Cut-Rate Quarterback*,
1977; and *Thin Ice*, 1978.

Gault has also contributed numerous short stories
to such periodicals as *Grit* and *Saturday Evening Post*.
He's been given several awards for his work including the
Edgar Allan Poe Award from the Mystery Writers of
America in 1952; a Boys' Club of America award in 1957;
an award from the Southern California Council on
Literature for Children and Young People in 1968; and a
Lifetime Achievement Award from Private Eye Writers
of America.

He is married to Virginia Kaprelian and the couple
have two children.

GEHRMANN, BERNARD JOHN, (1880-1953) a U. S.
Representative from Wisconsin; born in Gnesen, near
Koenigsberg, East Prussia, Germany February 13, 1880;
attended the common schools in Germany; in 1893 immigrated to the United States with his parents, who settled
in Chicago, Ill.; employed in a packing plant in Chicago
and later learned the printing trade on a German-language
daily newspaper; attended night school; moved to
Wisconsin and settled on a farm near Neillsville, Clark
County, in 1896 and engaged in agricultural pursuits; moved to a farm near Mellen, Ashland County, in 1915; clerk
of the school board 1916-1934, town assessor 1916-1921, and
chairman of the town board 1921-1932; conducted farmers'

institutes throughout the State for the University of Wisconsin College of Agriculture 1920-1933; served in the State assembly 1927-1933; delegate to the Republican National Convention in 1932; member of the State senate in 1933 and 1934; elected as a Progressive to the Seventy-fourth and to the three succeeding Congresses (January 3, 1935-January 3, 1943); unsuccessful candidate for reelection in 1942 to the Seventy-Eighth Congress; engaged in work for the United States Department of Agriculture from January 1943 until April 1945; elected to the Wisconsin assembly in 1946, 1948, 1950, and 1952; elected to the State senate in 1954 for the term ending in January 1957; died in Mellen, Wis., July 12, 1953; interment in Mellen Union Cemetery.

GOODLAND, WALTER S. (1862-1947), Wisconsin's thirtieth governor, was born in Sharon, Wisconsin on December 22, 1862, the son of John and Carolina (Clark) Goodland. He attended Lawrence College for one year, then found work as a school teacher in the rural area near Appleton, Wisconsin. In 1883, he married Christena Lewis. They had four children.

After teaching school for five years, Goodland studied law in his father's law office. He was admitted to the Wisconsin Bar in 1886, and soon moved to Wakefield, Michigan where he started a law practice. He also established a newspaper, *The Wakefield Bulletin,* which failed when the town was destroyed by fire a year later. His wife Christena died in 1896, and two years later he married her sister, Annie Lewis. He had one daughter by his second marriage. Also in 1888, Goodland founded the newspaper, *Ironwood Times,* which remained in print until 1895. He served as postmaster of Ironwood until 1899 when he moved to Beloit, Wisconsin and became part owner and publisher of the *Daily News.* In 1900, he became editor and publisher of the *Racine Times,* and in 1915, president of Call Publishing Company which owned the Racine paper.

While in Racine, Goodland served as president of the Water Commission for twelve years, and mayor of the city for one term. He was elected to the State Senate in 1926, and won reelection in 1930. His wife Annie died in December of that year, and three years later, he married Madge (Roach) Risney. In 1938, under Governor Heil, Goodland was elected Lieutenant Governor. He was reelected to the office in 1940 and 1942. Shortly before inauguration in 1942, Governor-elect Loomis died of a heart attack, and the Supreme Court named Goodland Acting Governor. He was elected to the office in 1944, and again in 1946. During his administration, Goodland took advantage of World War II prosperity to build up the state treasury. Many of these funds were devoted to rehabilitation and veterans' benefits. Goodland was a strong supporter of the Thomson Anti-Gambling Act of 1945. He also helped develop a fifteen-point program to improve conditions for state employees. Walter Goodland died on March 12, 1947, just after the start of his third term as governor.

GREGORY, HORACE VICTOR (1898-1982), was a professor, author and a prominent American poet.

Born in Milwaukee, Wisconsin on April 10, 1898, he was sickly as a child and was tutored at home during his grammar school years.

During high school he attended German-English Academy in Milwaukee and he spent his summers studying at the Milwaukee School of Fine Arts. He later enrolled at the University of Wisconsin, receiving a B.A. in 1923.

Gregory spent most of his adult life as a poet, critic, editor, and author living both in New York and Europe. He was also a lecturer in poetry, as well as an instructor in advanced writing at Sarah Lawrence College from 1934 to 1960.

Some of his books include: *Pilgrim of the Apocalypse: A Critical Study of D.H. Lawrence*, 1933; *The Shield of Achilles: Essays on Beliefs in Poetry*, 1944; (with wife Marya Zaturenska) *A History of American Poetry, 1900-1940*, 1946; *Amy Lowell: Portrait of the Poet in Her Time*, 1958; *The World of James McNeill Whistler*, 1959; and *Dorothy Richardson: An Adventure in Self-Discovery* 1967.

Some of his poetry works are: *Chelsea Rooming House*, 1930; *A Wreath for Margery*, 1933; *Chorus for Survival*, 1935; *Medusa in Gramercy Park*, 1961; and *Another Look*, 1976.

Gregory contributed a number of poems and critical reviews to various periodicals such as *Vanity Fair*, *Atlantic*, *New Republic*, and *Nation*, among others. He also wrote introductions for books including *Columbia Poetry*, 1940; *Alice's Adventures in Wonderland, (and) Through the Looking-Glass* ; and *e.e. cummings: A Selection of Poems*, 1966.

Awards and honors he received through the years were: Lyric Prize, *Poetry* magazine, 1928; Levinson

Award, 1936; Russell Loines Award for Poetry, from the National Institute of Arts and Letters, 1942; and the Bollingen Prize from Yale University Library, 1965; among others.

Gregory's wife Marya was also a poet and the couple had two children. He died on March 11, 1982.

GRENE, MARJORIE GLICKSMAN (1910-?), is an educator and author.

Born in Milwaukee, Wisconsin on December 13, 1910, she received her education at Wellesley College where she was awarded a B.A. degree in 1931. She then did her graduate work at the University of Freiburg in 1931-32 and at the University of Heidelberg in 1932-33. She earned both her M.A. and Ph.D. degrees from Radcliffe College.

She began her teaching career at Monticello College in 1936 and the following year became an instructor in philosophy at the University of Chicago where she taught until 1944. In 1957 she traveled to England to work as a research assistant at the University of Manchester for a year, studied on a research fellow in education at the University of Leeds during 1958, then began lecturing in philosophy during 1959-60. She did the same at The Queen's University of Belfast in Northern Ireland from 1960 to 1965. She returned to the U.S. in 1965 and was a professor of philosophy at the University of California, Davis until 1978, becoming professor emeritus in the latter year.

She has also been a visiting professor at various schools throughout the country, including: the University of Texas at Austin, 1967-68; Boston University, 1972; Temple University, 1979, Rutgers University, 1979; University of California, Berkeley, 1980; Yale University, 1980; and State University of New York, 1986.

She has written several philosophy books, including: *Dreadful Freedom: A Critique of Existentialism*, 1948; *Martin Heidegger*, 1957; *A Portrait of Aristotle*, 1963; *Approaches to a Philosophical Biology*, 1968; *Sartre*, 1973; *Philosophy in and out of Europe*, 1976; and *Descartes*, 1985.

She has also worked as editor on a number of books such as: (With Thomas Vernor Smith) *From Descartes to Kant: Readings in the Philosophy of the Renaissance and Enlightenment*, 1940; *Toward a Unity of Knowledge* 1969; *The Anatomy of Knowledge*, 1969; and *Interpretations of Life and Mind: Essays around the Problem of Reduction*, 1971; among others.

She has been a member of various organizations, including the Metaphysical Society of America; the Society for Phenomenology and Existential Philosophy; and the American Philosophical Association.

Grene is divorced and has two children.

GRIFFIN, MICHAEL, (1842- 1899) a U. S. Representative from Wisconsin; born in County Glare, Ireland, September 9, 1842; immigrated with his parents to Canada in 1847 and to Ohio in 1851; moved to Wisconsin in 1856 and settled in Newport, Soak County; attended the common schools of Ohio and Wisconsin; enlisted in the Union Army September 11, 1861, as a private in Company E, Twelfth Regiment, Wisconsin Volunteer Infantry, and served until the close of the war, attaining the rank of first lieutenant; moved to Kilbourn City, Wis., in 1865; studied law; was admitted to the bar in 1868 and commenced practice in Kilbourn City; cashier of the Bank of Kilbourn 1871-1876; member of the County Board of Columbia County, Wis., in 1874 and 1875; member of the State assembly in 1876; moved to Eau Claire, Wis., in 1876; city attorney of Eau Claire in 1878 and 1879; served in the State senate in 1880 and 1881; department commander of the Grand Army of the Republic in 1887 and 1888; elected as a Republican to the Fifty-third Congress to fill the vacancy caused by the death of George B. Show and at the same election to the Fifty-fourth Congress; reelected to the Fifty-fifth Congress and served from November 5, 1894, to March 3, 1899; was not a candidate for renomination in 1898; appointed chairman of the State tax commission by Governor Schofield May 28, 1899; died in Eau Claire, Wis., December 29, 1899; interment in Forest Hill Cemetery.

GUENTHER, RICHARD WILLIAM, (1845- a U. S. Representative from Wisconsin; born in Potsdam, Prussia, on November 30, 1845; received a collegiate training and was graduated from the Royal Pharmacy in Potsdam; immigrated to the United States in July 1866 and settled in New York City; moved to Oshkosh, Wis., in 1867 and engaged in the drug business; State treasurer of Wisconsin 1878-1882; elected as a Republican to the Forty-seventh and to the three succeeding Congresses (March 4, 1881-March 3, 1889); appointed by President Harrison consul general at Mexico City January 28, 1890, and served until May 21, 1893, when he resigned; appointed by President McKinley consul general at Frankfort on the Main, Germany, November 11, 1898, and served until July 21, 1910;

appointed by President Taft consul general at Cape Town, Africa, May 4, 1910, and served until his death in Oshkosh, Wis., April 5, 1913; interment in Riverside Cemetery.

H

HARVEY, LOUIS POWELL (1820-1862), seventh governor of Wisconsin (1862), was born in East Haddam, Connecticut, July 22, 1820. In 1828 his family moved to Strongville, Ohio. At the age of seventeen he entered Western Reserve College, at Hudson, Ohio, but after two years was compelled to leave it on account of ill-health. He then engaged in teaching, which he followed in Kentucky, and, subsequently, as a tutor in Woodward College, Cincinnati. In the autumn of 1841 he located in Southport, now Kenosha, Wisconsin, where he opened a school. Two years later he also assumed editorial charge of the Southport "American," a Whig newspaper, and was for a time postmaster of the place. In 1847 he moved to Clinton, which he represented the same year in the first state constitutional convention of Wisconsin. In 1851 he went to Waterloo, engaging in manufacturing and mercantile pursuits. He was a member of the State Senate, 1854-57, and during his last term served as president *pro tem*. In 1859 he was elected Secretary of State, and after filling this office for two years, was elected by the Republican party Chief-Magistrate of Wisconsin. He entered this position January 6, 1862, and served until his tragic death, when Lieutenant-Governor Edward Salomon became governor under the constitution. Governor Harvey was also a member of the board of regents of the state university, and was active in shaping the educational system of the state. He was a man of superior ability, a clear insight into public affairs, with a reputation for integrity and fidelity to truth and duty, and "no man in Wisconsin ever took the gubernatorial chair with a brighter prospect of an honorable career before him." He was married in 1847 to Cordelia A. Perrine. After the battle of Shiloh, in which Wisconsin troops had met with terrible losses, Governor Harvey returned to the scene of suffering with supplies for the relief of the wounded. While returning home he fell overboard from a steamboat near Savannah, Tennessee, and drowned in the Tennessee River, April 19, 1862.

HAVIGHURST, WALTER EDWIN (1901-?), is an educator and novelist.

Born in Appleton, Wisconsin on November 28, 1901, he first attended the University of Denver where he received an A.B. degree in 1924. He then went to London for a year to study at King's College during 1925-26, and returned to the States to finish his education at Columbia University where he was awarded an A.M. degree in 1928.

That same year, he began his career as an assistant professor at Miami University. In 1935 he was named associate professor and continued to move up the ranks to professor of English, (1942), research professor (1949), Regents professor (1968) and research professor emeritus (1969).

During his life he has written numerous books, some of which include: *Pier 17*, 1935; *The Quiet Shore* 1937; *No Homeward Course*, 1941; *Approach to America*, 1942; *Signature of Time*, 1949; *Great Plains*, 1951; *Annie Oakley of the Wild West*, 1954; *First Book of the Oregon Trail*, 1960; *First Book of the California Gold Rush*, 1960; and *Ohio: A Bicentennial History*.

Havighurst has been given several awards, such as the Ohioana Library Association Medal, 1946-1950, Friends of American Writers Award, 1947, Association for State and Local History Award, 1956, and the History Prize from the Society of Midland Authors, 1971.

In describing his work, Havighurst once mentioned in an interview that some of his earlier writing was inspired by his travels as a merchant seaman. However, his later material was based on his Midwestern upbringing. "I realized that my own background, of midland America, was for me the inexhaustible subject," he said. He spoke of "wanting to recall the Midwest of past times while trying to understand its ever-changing present. This is the background I am most at home with, and toward which my writing seems to gravitate."

Havighurst was married to writer Marion Boyd who died in 1974.

HEIL, JULIUS PETER (1876-1949), twenty-ninth governor of Wisconsin, was born on July 24, 1876 in Duesmond an der Mosel, Germany, the son of Franz and Barbara (Krebs) Heil. His family came to Wisconsin in 1881 and he attended Mill Valley rural school until the age of twelve. In 1888, he began work as an assistant in a general store. Later he went to Milwaukee where he worked a series of jobs including that of drill press operator, newpaper vendor on trains, streetcar conductor, boiler fireman and assistant blacksmith. He also worked as as rail joints salesman, a job that took him to many parts of the world. In 1900, he married Elizabeth Conrad. They had one son.

He settled in Milwaukee again in 1901 and established the Heil Rail Joint Company, which later became known as Heil Company. He ran for Milwaukee city treasurer in 1908, but lost the election, and devoted himself to his business until 1938, when he made a reentry into politics with his candidacy for governor. A Republican, he won against Progressive Philip La Follette who was running for an unprecedented fourth term. Once in office, Heil began to reorganize state government, using business methods. He created a Motor Vehicle Department, and the controversial Division of Departmental Research, and consolidated the Department of Welfare. Reelected in 1940, he created the State Guard to replace the National Guard, during World War II. He also signed into law the Industrial Peace Act. He ran for a third term in 1942, but lost to Orland Loomis.

Heil returned to Heil Company, where he was made president, a position he held until 1946, when he turned it over to his son, Joseph. He subsequently served as chairman of the board for the company, until his death on November 30, 1949.

HENNEY, CHARLES WILLIAM FRANCIS, (1884-1969) a U. S. Representative from Wisconsin; born on a farm near Dunlap, Harrison County, Iowa, February 2, 1884; attended the district school and Denison (Iowa) Normal School; taught in a district school in Crawford County, Iowa, 1902-1905; was graduated from the pharmacy department of Fremont (Nebr.) Normal School in 1906 and from the medical department of Northwestern University, Chicago, Ill., in 1910; moved to Portage, Columbia County, Wis., in 1912 and commenced the practice of medicine; delegate to all Democratic State conventions from 1920 to 1936; delegate to Democratic National Conventions in 1936, 1940, 1944, and 1948; member of the Portage City Park Commission 1925-1933; chief of staff of St. Savior's Hospital, Portage City, Wis., in 1926 and 1927; elected as a Democrat to the Seventy-third Congress (March 4, 1933January 3, 1935); unsuccessful candidate for reelection in 1934 to the Seventy-fourth Congress; resumed the practice of medicine and surgery; died in Portage, Wis., November 16, 1969; interment in St. Mary's Catholic Cemetery.

HENRY, ROBERT KIRKLAND, (February 9, 1890-November 20, 1946) a U. S. Representative from Wisconsin; born in Jefferson, Jefferson County, Wis.; attended the public schools of his native city and the University of Wisconsin at Madison; engaged in the banking business; served as State treasurer 1931-1935; member of the Jefferson Municipal Water and Light Commission from November 7, 1939, to December 1, 1944; member of the State Banking Commission 1940-1944; elected as a Republican to the Seventy-ninth Congress and served from January 3, 1945, until his death; had been reelected to the Eightieth Congress; died in Madison, Wis.; interment in Greenwood Cemetery, Jefferson, Wis.

HUDD, THOMAS RICHARD, (1835-1896) a U. S. Representative from Wisconsin; born in Buffalo, N.Y., October 2, 1835; moved with his mother to Chicago, Ill., in 1842 and to Appleton, Wis., in 1853; attended the common schools and Lawrence University, Appleton, Wis.; studied law; commenced practice in Appleton, Wis.; district attorney of Outagamie County in 1856 and 1857; served in the State senate in 1862, 1863, 1876-1879, 1882, 1883, and 1885; moved to Green Bay in 1868 and continued the practice of law; member of the State assembly in 1868 and 1875; city attorney of Green Bay in 1873 and 1874; delegate to the Democratic National Convention in 1880; elected as a Democrat to the Forty-ninth Congress to fill the vacancy caused by the death of Joseph Rankin; reelected to the Fiftieth Congress and served from March 8, 1886, to March 3, 1889; chairman, Committee on Expenditures in the Department of the Interior (Fiftieth Congress); did not seek renomination in 1888; resumed the practice of law; died in Green Bay, Wis., on June 22, 1896; interment in Woodlawn Cemetery.

HULL, MERLIN, (1870-1953) a U. S. Representative from Wisconsin; born in Warsaw, Kosciusko County, Ind., December 18, 1870; attended Gale College, Galesville, Wis., De Pauw University, Greencastle, Ind., and Columbian (now George Washington) University, Washington, D.C.; studied law; was admitted to the bar in 1894 and commenced practice in Black River Falls, Wis.; publisher of the Jackson County Journal 1904-1926 and of the Banner-Journal 1926-1953; also engaged in agricultural pursuits; district attorney of Jackson County 1907-1909; member of the Wisconsin assembly 1909-1915, serving as speaker in 1913; secretary of state of Wisconsin 1917-1921; elected as a Republican to the Seventy-first Congress (March 4, 1929-March 3, 1931); unsuccessful candidate for renomination in 1930 and unsuccessful Independent candidate for reelection to the Seventy-second Congress; resumed former business pursuits; elected as a Progressive to the Seventy-fourth and to the five succeeding Congresses, and as a Republican to the Eightieth and to the three succeeding Congresses and served from January 3, 1935, until his death in La Crosse, Wis., May 17, 1953; interment in Oak Grove Cemetery.

HUMPHREY, HERMAN LEON, (1830-1887) a U. S. Representative from Wisconsin; born in Candor, Tioga County, N.Y., March 14, 1830; attended the common schools and also the Cortland Academy for one year; became a clerk in Ithaca, N.Y.; after several years in business he studied law; was admitted to the bar in July 1854 and in January 1855 moved to Hudson, Wis., where he commenced practice; appointed district attorney of St. Croix County; appointed county judge to fill a vacancy in the fall of 1860 and in the spring of 1861 was elected for the full term of four years, but resigned that office in February 1862; served in the State senate in 1862 and 1863; mayor of Hudson one year; elected in the spring of 1866 judge of the eighth judicial circuit of Wisconsin and reelected in 1872; elected as a Republican to the Forty-fifth, Forty-sixth, and Forty-seventh Congresses (March 4, 1877-March 3, 1883); unsuccessful candidate for renomination; resumed the practice of law in Hudson, St. Croix County, Wis.; member of the State assembly in 1887; died in Hudson, Wis., June 10, 1902; interment in Willow River Cemetery.

HUSTING, PAUL OSCAR, (1866-1917) a U. S. Senator from Wisconsin; born in Fond do Lac, Fond do Lac County, Wis., April 25, 1866; moved with his parents to Mayville, Wis., in 1876; attended the public schools and the law school of the University of Wisconsin at Madison; was admitted to the bar in 1895 and commenced practice in Mayville, Wis.; district attorney of Dodge County 1902-1906; member, State senate 1907-1913; elected as a Democrat to the United States Senate in 1914 and served from March 4, 1915, until his accidental death while duck hunting on Rush Lake, near Picketts, Wis., on October 21, 1917; chairman, Committee to Investigate Trespassers Upon Indian Land

(Sixty-fourth and Sixty-fifth Congresses), Committee on Fisheries (Sixty-fifth Congress); interment in Graceland Cemetery, Mayville, Wis.

J

JOLLIET, LOUIS, (1645-1700), explorer, was born at Quebec, Canada, September 21, 1645, the son of John Jolliet, a wagon-maker, and Mary d'Abancour. He was educated in the Jesuit college for the priesthood, receiving minor orders in 1662. Subsequently he became a trader and explorer. In 1669 he was sent by Talon, the Intendant of Canada, to discover the copper mines of Lake Superior, but was unsuccessful on this mission.

On account of his knowledge and experience, however, Jolliet was recommeneded by Talon as a fit leader for the expedition that Frontenac, Governor of Canada, was about to send out to explore the Mississippi River, which, up to this time, was supposed to empty into the South Sea. James Marquette, a Jesuit missionary at St. Esprit, La Pointe, Lake Superior, was chosen as Jolliet's priest-associate. The exploring party, consisting of seven Frenchmen, set out from St. Ignace on May 17, 1672. After obtaining all possible information from the Indians, Jolliet made a map of the proposed route, which, revised by Marquette, was afterward published in *Shea's Discovery and Exploration of the Mississippi Valley*.

On June 7, 1673, the explorers arrived at an Indian town, marking the extreme western limit of French discoveries, and after descending the Wisconsin and Illinois rivers they entered the Mississippi, June 17, 1673. Continuing their course, they reached the mouth of the Missouri, afterward coming to a village of Arkansas Indians, at 33° 40' north latitude, and within ten days' journey of the river's mouth. This proved, beyond a doubt, that the Mississippi emptied into the Gulf of Mexico, and on July 17, 1673, the explorers began to tediously retrace their way, arriving at the frontier mission on Green Bay, in September, 1673.

Here Marquette remained to recover his health, while Jolliet made his way back to Quebec. In the rapids of La Chine, near Montreal, his canoe and all his maps and papers were lost. The account of the journey is, therefore, taken from the journal of Marquette, although Jolliet, from memory, reproduced his discoveries in a small map that was later kept in the Chart office in Paris.

In 1679 Jolliet resumed his occupation of trader and journeyed to Hudson Bay by way of the Saguenay. Up to this time he had had no substantial acknowledgment of his services, or his plans for colonizing the fertile valley he had discovered, but about 1680 he was granted the island of Anticosti. Here, ten years later, his entire possessions were destroyed by the English, and his wife, Clare Frances Brissot, whom he had married on October 7, 1675, was taken prisoner. The attack was made in 1690 by Sir William Phips, who was on his way to attack Quebec.

Jolliet again turned adventurer, and in 1694 explored the coast of Labrador under the auspices of a company formed for whale and seal fishing. On Jolliet's return, Governor Frontenac made him royal pilot for the St. Lawrence, and in 1697 granted him the seigniory of Jolliet south of Quebec. He succeeded Franquelin, a young engineer, as hydrographer to the king in Quebec, Canada. The historian Parkman said: "From what we know of Joliet, there is nothing that reveals any salient or distinctive trait of character, any especial breadth of view of boldness of design. He appears simply a merchant, well-educated, courageous, hardy and enterprising". Although the honor of having first explored the greater part of the Mississippi River would seem unquestionably to be his, the matter has long been disputed, with many authorities declaring in favor of De Soto and La Salle. Jolliet died in Canada in May, 1700, and was buried on one of the Mignan Islands.

K

KADING, CHARLES AUGUST, (1874-1956) a U. S. Representative from Wisconsin; born in Lowell, Dodge County, Wis., January 14, 1874; attended the country schools, Lowell graded school, Horicon High School, and the University of Wisconsin at Madison; was graduated from the law department of Valparaiso University, Valparaiso, Ind., in 1900; was admitted to the bar the same year and commenced practice in Watertown, Wis.; also interested in agricultural pursuits; city attorney of Watertown 1905-1912; district attorney for Dodge County, Wis., 1906-1912; mayor of Watertown 1914-1916; elected as a Republican to the Seventieth, Seventy-first, and Seventy-second Congresses (March 4, 1927-March 3, 1933); unsuccessful candidate for renomination in 1932; resumed the practice of law; died in Watertown, Wis., June 19, 1956; interment in Oak Hill Cemetery.

KALTENBORN, HANS VON (1878-1965) was a highly-respected news commentator for over twenty-five years.

Born in Milwaukee, Wisconsin on July 9, 1878, he graduated *cum laude* from Harvard in 1909. However, he began working as a newspaper writer with the *Merrill News* at the age of fifteen. He joined the 4th Wisconsin Volunteer Infantry as a first sergeant during the Spanish-American War and acted as war correspondent for several Wisconsin newspapers.

He then left for Europe, traveling on a cattle boat, and worked for years as a foreign correspondent. It was after he returned to the United States that he decided to pursue his college education by enrolling in Harvard University. The year after his graduation, he began working as a reporter for the *Brooklyn Eagle* and eventually became associate editor. Later, with the newspaper's help, he began doing live radio broadcasts on local stations.

Kaltenborn went national when he signed on with the Columbia Broadcasting System as chief news commentator in 1929. He stayed with CBS until 1940, when he switched to the National Broadcasting Company. Through the years, he worked in both radio and television, compiling impressive accomplishments such as broadcasting while hidden in a haystack during the Spanish Civil War, with the sound of machine gun fire in the background, or his marathon broadcasting session in 1938 as the Munich crisis was taking place. During the latter, he reported the news over 100 times in 18 days, never leaving the station so that he could relay the latest on the delicate negotiations between British Prime Minister Neville Chamberlain and Adolf Hitler. During World War II, he traveled throughout Europe and the Pacific to do his broadcasts.

He finally retired from broadcasting in 1955, involving himself in the occasional event such as the reelection of Dwight D. Eisenhower. He wrote several books, including: *We Look at the World*, 1930; *Kaltenborn Edits the News*, 1937; *I Broadcast the Crisis*, 1938; *Kaltenborn Edits the War News*, 1942; *Europe Now*, 1945; plus his autobiography *Fifty Fabulous Years*, 1950.

Kaltenborn was honored with awards such as: a Radio Certificate of Merit by the National Federation of Press Women, DuPont award, 1945; First Award for news analysis, Radio Institute of Ohio State University, 1945; and a gold plaque in 1936 for the best foreign radio reporting during the Spanish Civil War.

Kaltenborn married Baroness Olga von Nordenflycht in 1910 and the couple had two children. He died on June 14, 1965.

KASTENMEIER, ROBERT WILLIAM, (January 24, 1924-) a U. S. Representative from Wisconsin; born in Beaver Dam, Dodge County, Wis.; attended the public schools of Beaver Dam; Carleton College, Northfield, Minn.; University of Wisconsin, LL.B., 1952; was admitted to the bar the same year and commenced the practice of law in Watertown, Wis.; entered the United States Army as a private in February 1943; served in the Philippines and was discharged as a first lieutenant on August 15, 1946; War Department branch office director, claims service, in the Philippines 1946-1948; elected justice of the peace for Jefferson and Dodge Counties in 1955 and served until 1959; elected as a Democrat to the Eightysixth and to the fourteen succeeding Congresses (January 3, 1959-January 3, 1989); is a resident of Sun Prairie, Wis.

KEEFE, FRANK BATEMAN, (September 23, 1887-February 5, 1952) a U. S. Representative from Wisconsin, born in Winneconne, Winnebago County, Wis.;

attended the public schools; was graduated from Oshkosh (Wis.) State Normal School in 1906 and from the law department of the University of Michigan at Ann Arbor in 1910; teacher in the schools at Viroqua, Vernon County, Wis., in 1906 and 1907; was admitted to the bar in 1910 and commenced practice in Oshkosh, Wis.; prosecuting attorney of Winnebago County, Wis., 1922-1928; vice president and director of an Oshkosh bank; elected as a Republican to the Seventy-sixth and to the five succeeding Congresses (January 3, 1939-January 3, 1951); was not a candidate for renomination in 1950; resumed the practice of law; died in Neenah, Wis.; interment in Lakeview Memorial Park, Oshkosh, Wis.

KENNAN, GEORGE FROST (1904-?) is a diplomat and historian.

Born in Milwaukee, Wisconsin on February 16, 1904, he received an A.B. degree from Princeton in 1925. He also studied at the Berlin Seminary for Oriental Languages, graduating in 1930.

Kennan began his career as a Foreign Service Officer at the U. S. Department of State in 1926. He served in several countries such as Berlin, Vienna, Geneva, Hamburg and Moscow from 1927 until 1939. He was named first secretary of the U.S. legation in Berlin in 1940, but was repatriated in 1942. The following year, he was counselor of the American delegation to the European Advisory Commission in London and then became minister/counselor in Moscow. In 1947, he was named director of the State Department's policy planning staff in Washington, D.C., becoming their counselor in 1949. He spent the year 1952 as ambassador to the U.S.S.R. and retired from the Foreign Service in 1953. He held one more government job in 1961 when he served as ambassador to Yugoslavia.

Kennan was a lecturer for the Charles R. Walgreen Foundation at the University of Chicago in 1951, and at Princeton University in 1954. In addition, he has been a member of the Institute for Advanced Study at Princeton in 1950 and 1953, becoming a professor in 1964.

His writings include: *American Diplomacy, 1900-1950*, 1951; *Realities of American Foreign Policy*, 1954; *Das amerikanisch russische Verhaltnis*, 1954; *Russia Leaves the War*, first volume of *Soviet-American Relations, 1917-1920*, 1956; *Russia, the Atom, and the West*, 1958; and *On Dealing With the Communist World*, 1964; among others.

Kennan has been honored with several prestigious awards during his career as a diplomat, including: the Freedom House Award for *American Diplomacy*, in 1951; the Pulitzer Prize in history, in 1957; the National Book Award, Bancroft Prize, and Francis Parkman Prize, for *Russia Leaves the War* ; and a second Pulitzer Prize in 1968 for his book *Memoirs, 1925-1950*, 1967. (The second volume of his autobiography, *Memoirs, 1950-1963* was published in 1972.)

Kennan is married to Annelise Sorensen and the couple have four children.

KERSTEN, CHARLES JOSEPH, (1902-1972) a U. S. Representative from Wisconsin; born in Chicago, Ill., May 26, 1902; was graduated from Marquette University College of Law, Milwaukee, Wis., in 1925 and was admitted to the bar the same year; commenced the practice of law in Milwaukee, Wis., in 1928; first assistant district attorney of Milwaukee County 1937-1943; elected as a Republican to the Eightieth Congress (January 3, 1947-January 3, 1949); unsuccessful candidate for reelection in 1948 to the Eighty-first Congress; elected to the Eighty-second and Eighty-third Congresses (January 3, 1951-January 3, 1955); chairman, Select Committee on Communist Aggression (Eighty-third Congress); unsuccessful candidate for reelection in 1954 to the Eighty-fourth Congress; White House consultant on psychological warfare, 1955- 1956; unsuccessful candidate for nomination in 1956 to the Eighty-fifth Congress; resumed the practice of law until his death October 31, 1972, in Milwaukee, Wis.; interment in Holy Cross Cemetery.

KIMBALL, AIANSON MELLEN, (1827- 1913) a U. S. Representative from Wisconsin; born in Buxton, York County, Maine, March 12, 1827; pursued academic studies; moved to Wisconsin in 1852 and engaged in agricultural and mercantile pursuits; served in the State senate in 1863 and 1864; elected as a Republican to the Forty-fourth Congress (March 4, 1875-March 3, 1877); was an unsuccessful candidate for election in 1876 to the Forty-fifth Congress; engaged in the lumbering business; delegate to the Republican National Convention in 1884; died in Pine River, Waushara County, Wis., May 26, 1913; interment in Pine River Cemetery.

KING, FRANK O. (1883-1969), was a cartoonist known for his famous cartoon strip, *Gasoline Alley.*

Born in Cashon, Wisconsin on April 9, 1883, King attended the Chicago Academy of Fine Arts. However, by the time he decided to pursue his studies at the academy, he had been working as a cartoonist at the *Minneapolis Times* for five years, beginning in 1901 when he was eighteen.

In 1906, he worked for a short time at an advertising agency then became a staff member of the *Chicago Examiner.* He stayed until 1909, then switched to the *Chicago Tribune* where he had his own weekly cartoon.

In 1919, he came up with a comic strip about automobiles, entitled *Gasoline Alley* which built a solid following as the years went by, mostly due to the fact that the characters were allowed to get older. People enjoyed following their lives as they married and had children, and then grandchildren. The strip was syndicated in later years and appeared in hundreds of newspapers throughout the country.

King died on June 24, 1969 in Winter Park, Florida.

KLECZKA, JOHN CASIMIR, (1885-1959) a U. S. Representative from Wisconsin; born in Milwaukee, Wis., on May 6, 1885; attended the parochial schools; was graduated from Marquette University, Milwaukee, Wis., in 1905; took postgraduate courses at Catholic University at Washington, D.C., and at the University of Wisconsin at Madison; studied law; was admitted to the bar in 1909 and commenced practice in Milwaukee; served in the State senate 1909-1911; delegate to the Republican National Convention in 1912; commissioner of the circuit court of Milwaukee County 1914-1918; major judge advocate in the United States Army Reserves after the First World War; elected as a Republican to the Sixty-sixth and Sixty-seventh Congresses (March 4, 1919-March 3, 1923); did not seek renomination in 1922 but returned to the practice of law; elected circuit court judge in 1930 and served until his retirement due to ill health in 1953; appointed a conciliation judge and court commissioner by the circuit judges in 1957 and served until his death; died in Milwaukee, Wis., April 21, 1959; interment in St. Adalbert's Cemetery.

KNATHS, (OTTO) KARL (1891-1971) was a painter and an artist.

Born in Eau Claire, Wisconsin on October 21, 1891, he was a student at the Art Institute of Chicago for five years.

His early work was in the expressionistic style, but he later painted scenes inspired by landscapes near his home in Provincetown. Around 1930, he adopted a more abstract style, influenced by cubism.

His work has hung in several prestigious forums, including: the Metropolitan Museum; the Phillips Memorial Gallery; the Gallery of Living Art; the Detroit Museum; the Whitney Museum; the New York Museum of Modern Art; and the Art Institute of Chicago.

He has received numerous awards for his paintings, such as the Norman Wait Harris silver medal from the Art Institute of Chicago, in 1928; a medal of the Boston Tercentenary; First Prize by the Carnegie Institute, in 1946; First Prize from the Metropolitan Museum, in 1950; the Brandeis University creative art award, in 1961; and the Audubon Art award, in 1964; among others.

Knaths was married to Helene Weinrich in 1922. He died on March 9, 1971.

KNOWLES, WARREN P. (1908-), Wisconsin's thirty-sixth governor, was born on August 19, 1908 in River Falls, Wisconsin, the son of William P. Knowles, II and Anna (Deneen) Knowles. He attended Carleton College in Minnesota, and the University of Wisconsin, where he graduated with a law degree in 1933. He was admitted to the Wisconsin Bar and became a partner in a law firm in New Richmond, Wisconsin.

Knowles was elected to the New Richmond County Board in 1935, and served five years. In 1940 he became a state senator, but his time in the State Senate was interrupted by World War II. He entered the U.S. Navy and took part in the invasions of Attu, Normandy and southern France. In 1946 he was discharged with the rank of lieutenant and returned to the State Senate where he remained until 1953, serving as Majority Floor Leader for a time. Meanwhile, in 1943, he married Dorothy C. Guidry, a union that ended in divorce in 1968.

He continued his political career in 1954, when he was elected Lieutenant Governor of Wisconsin. Twice reelected, he served until 1964, when he won the governorship in a race against incumbent John W. Reynolds. During his administration, Knowles attempted to curb what he called excessive spending. He promoted the development of industry and other economic expansion in the state. He was reelected in 1966 and 1968. His later terms were concerned with the expansion of the state college system, vocational education, improvements to highways, water pollution control, and the provision of new outdoor recreation areas. He appointed the Kellett Commission to make recommendations on how to reorganize state government and control the state debt. He also created the Tarr Task Force to advise on fiscal management. Knowles declined to seek reelection in 1970. He became the chairman of the board for Inland Financial Corporation in 1971. Since leaving the governorship, he has also remained active in philanthropic and civic activities.

KOHLER, WALTER J. (1875-1940), twenty-sixth governor of Wisconsin, was born on March 3, 1875 in Sheboygan, Wisconsin, the son of John and Lilly (Vollrath) Kohler. His father was the founder of Kohler Company, which manufactured farm tools, and at the age of fifteen, Walter left school to work in his father's business. He married Charlotte H. Schroeder in 1900, and they had four sons. Two days after his wedding, his father died, and Walter became superintendent of the Kohler Company plant. In the years that followed, he served as president and chairman of the board for the company.

In 1916, Kohler was chosen as a presidental elector. This led him to become more involved in politics. In 1918, Governor Philipp appointed him to the Board of Regents of the University of Wisconsin, a position he held until 1924. In 1928, he ran for governor on the Republican ticket and won. During his term in office, Kohler attempted to reorganize state administrative offices. He brought his own businesslike methods to this task, which resulted in the creation of the Department of the Budget and Accounts, the Bureau of Purchasing, the Bureau of Personnel, the Bureau of Engineering, and the Highway Commission. Kohler also expanded the Department of Agriculture and Markets, and added 800 positions to civil service.

Walter Kohler ran for a second term as governor in 1930, but lost in the primary to Philip La Follette. He ran again in 1932, beating La Follette in the primary, but losing to Democrat Albert Schmedeman in the general election. Kohler retired to business, which included concerns with Kohler Company, Vollrath Company, a Salt Lake City supply company, and several railroads. He died in River Bend, Wisconsin on April 21, 1940.

KOHLER, WALTER J., JR. (1904-1976), thirty-second governor of Wisconsin, was born in Sheboygan, Wisconsin on April 4, 1904, the son of Walter and Charlotte (Schroeder) Kohler. His father was Governor of Wisconsin. Walter Jr. attended Phillips Academy in Andover, Massachusetts and Yale University where he earned a Ph.B. degree in 1925. In 1932, he married Celeste McVoy Holden. They had two children.

After graduation from the university, Kohler began a job with the family business, working first in engineering and ceramic research and later in marketing and sales. He was named director of the Kohler Company in 1936, and in 1937 became its secretary. During World War II, Kohler was commissioned a lieutenant in the Naval Reserve. He was called to active duty, and served in the Western Pacific. After the war, he returned to Kohler Company where he was president from 1945-47. He then became president of the Vollrath Company, another family business.

In 1946, Kohler divorced his wife Celeste. He married Charlotte McAleer in 1948. That same year, he entered politics as a delegate-at-large at the Republican National Convention. He ran for governor in 1950 and won. He won reelection in 1952 and 1954, defeating Democrat William Proxmire both times, but by a slim margin in the second race. During his three terms as governor, Kohler sought to reduce state income tax, raise salaries for state employees, and continue Wisconsin's state building program. The Rosenberry Act, which reapportioned state voting districts on a population basis, was passed during his administration. In addition, a program to eradicate dairy cattle disease was begun in the state.

Kohler declined reelection in 1956, and the following year ran for the senate seat vacated by the death of Senator Joseph R. McCarthy. He met his Democratic adversary, William Proxmire, once again in the election, and this time Proxmire won. Kohler returned to his position as president of Vollrath Company. He died in Sheboygan on March 21, 1976.

KONOP, THOMAS FRANK, (1879-1964) a U. S. Representative from Wisconsin; born in Franklin, Wis., August 17, 1879; educated at Two Rivers High School, Oshkosh State Normal School, and Northern Illinois College of Law; was graduated from the law department of the University of Nebraska at Lincoln in 1904; was admitted to the bar in 1904 and commenced practice in Kewaunee, Wis.; district attorney of Kewaunee County 1905-1911;

moved to Green Bay, Wis., and practiced law 1915-1917; elected as a Democrat to the Sixty-second, Sixty-third, and Sixty-fourth Congresses (March 4, 1911-March 3, 1917); chairman, Committee on Expenditures on Public Buildings (Sixty-third and Sixty-fourth Congresses); unsuccessful candidate for reelection; resumed the practice of law in Madison, Wis.; member of the Wisconsin State Industrial Commission 1917-1922; member of State board of vocational education 1917-1922; moved to Milwaukee, Wis., and continued the practice of law in 1922 and 1923; dean of the College of Law of the University of Notre Dame 1923- 1941, and dean emeritus and professor of law until his retirement in 1950; resided in South Bend, Ind., until 1962; died in San Pierre, Ind., October 17, 1964; interment in Highland Cemetery, South Bend, Ind.

L

LA FOLLETTE, PHILLIP F. (1897-1965), Wisconsin's twenty-seventh governor, was born in Madison on May 8, 1897, the son of the famous Progressive leader and governor, Robert La Follette, and Belle (Case) La Follette. He attended the University of Wisconsin, graduating in 1919. During World War I, he served as a second lieutenant in the U.S. Army. He subsequently studied law in Washington, D.C. and at the University of Wisconsin Law School. He was admitted to the Bar, and entered his father's old law firm of La Follette, Rogers and Roberts. He married Isabel Bacon in 1923. They had three children.

In 1924, La Follette was elected District Attorney for Dane County. He served one term, and between 1926 and 1931 was a lecturer for the University of Wisconsin Law School. He ran for governor in 1930, winning against incumbent Walter Kohler in the primary, and Democrat Charles E. Hammersley in the general election. As governor, La Follette asked for greater government control over banks and the electric power industry. He also increased public works projects, especially highway building, and attempted to push through various anti-Depression measures. Although many of his proposals were blocked by a conservative Senate, he did see an Unemployment Compensation Act and a new State Labor Code passed. La Follette's Depression era administration was also marked by the failure of 116 banks, a fall in farm income of 33 percent in two years, and the closure of 1,500 businesses.

La Follette ran for a second term in 1932, but was defeated in the primary by his old adversary Walter Kohler. He responded to this defeat by throwing his support to Franklin D. Roosevelt and other Democrats. But rather than actually join the Democratic Party, he formed a third, Progressive Party, and returned in 1934 to win the gubernatorial election by a narrow margin. During his second administration he promoted programs for public power, public works and general relief, with little success from the conservative-controlled Senate. He won a third term in office in 1936, and with a new more progressive

77

group in the Legislature, forced passage of the Wisonsin Labor Relations Act. He founded the National Progressives of America in 1938, the same year he ran for a fourth term as governor. Fighting claims that some of the policies of the new progressives resembled those of European fascists, La Follette lost the election. Disheartened by his defeat, he returned to his law practice, and refused further association with Wisconsin politics. He died in Madison on August 10, 1965.

LA FOLLETTE, ROBERT MARION (1855-1921) (father of Robert Marion La Follette, Jr.), a U. S. Representative and a U. S. Senator from Wisconsin; born in Primrose, Dane County, Wis., June 14, 1855; graduated from the University of Wisconsin at Madison in 1879; studied law; was admitted to the bar in 1880 and commenced practice in Madison, Wis.; district attorney of Dane County 1880-1884; elected as a Republican to the Forty-ninth, Fiftieth, and Fifty-first Congresses (March 4, 1885-March 3, 1891); unsuccessful candidate for reelection in 1890 to the Fifty-second Congress; chairman, Committee on Expenditures in the Department of Agriculture (Fifty-first Congress); resumed the practice of law in Madison, Wis.; Governor of Wisconsin 1901-1906, when he resigned, having previously been elected Senator; elected as a Republican to the United States Senate on January 25, 1905, for the term beginning March 4, 1905, but did not assume these duties until later, preferring to continue as Governor; reelected in 1911, 1917, and 1923, and served from January 2, 1906, until his death; chairman, Committee on the Census (Sixty-first and Sixty-second Congress), Committee on Corporations Organized in the District of Columbia (Sixty-third through Sixty-fifth Congresses), Committee on Manufactures (Sixty-sixth through Sixty-eighth Congresses); one of the founders of the National Progressive Republican League and several times unsuccessfully sought the Republican and Progressive Party presidential nonimations; died in Washington, D.C., June 18, 1925; interment in Forest Hill Cemetery, Madison,

LAIRD, MELVIN ROBERT, (1922-) a U. S. Representative from Wisconsin; born in Omaha, Douglas County, Nebr., September 1, 1922; attended the public schools; B.A., Carleton College, Northfield, Minn., 1942; secretary-treasurer of a lumber company; enlisted in the United States Navy in May 1942 and served in the Pacific; awarded the Purple Heart; member of the State senate 1946-1952;

delegate to the Republican National Conventions in 1948, 1952, 1956, and 1960; elected as a Republican to the Eighty-third Congress; reelected to the eight succeeding Congresses and served from January 3, 1953, until his resignation January 21, 1969, to become Secretary of Defense and served in that capacity until January 29, 1973; domestic adviser to President Nixon, 1973-1974; senior counsellor for national and international affairs, Reader's Digest Association , 1974 to present is a resident of Marshfield, Wis.

LANDIS, CAROLE (1919-1948), born Frances Ridste, was a screen and stage actress, known as the original "sweater girl."

Born in Fairchild, Wisconsin on January 1, 1919, Landis began her movie career as an extra in the 1937 Marx Brothers movie, *A Day at the Races*. She continued to appear in numerous films, some of which include: *The Emperor's Candlesticks*, 1937; *Broadway Melody of 1938*, 1937; *A Star is Born*, 1937; *Blondes at Work*, 1938; *Men Are Such Fools*, 1938; *Moon Over Miami*, 1941; *My Gal Sal*, 1942; *Four Jills in a Jeep*, 1944; and *The Brass Monkey*, 1948.

Landis took her own life on July 5, 1948.

LASKER, MARY WOODARD (1900-?) is a highly respected philanthropist.

Born in Watertown, Wisconsin on November 30, 1900, she took fine arts courses at the University of Wisconsin for two years and then attended Radcliffe where she received her A.B. degree *cum laude* in 1923. She did her postgraduate work at Oxford University then returned to the United States and became an art dealer for the Reinhardt Galleries, a career she stayed in for seven years. She later admitted she left the art world because "I was tired of being in a business where numerically, few things were sold. I wanted to sell masses of things to masses of people. I found out that the things which people still bought in a depression were paper patterns." As such, she founded her own company, Hollywood Patterns.

In June of 1940, she married Albert D. Lasker who was the founder and president of Lord and Thomas, one of the first and most successful advertising agencies in America. Along with his agency, Lasker was an overwhelmingly generous philanthropist who gave millions to the University of Chicago for cancer research. He dissolved Lord and Thomas in 1942 in order to establish the Albert and Mary Lasker Foundation, which the couple said "underwrites pilot projects in basic research related to the major illnesses--now principally heart diseases, cancer, and mental illness--and also fosters dissemination of public information on the needs of medical research."

After Albert Lasker died in 1952, Mary Lasker continued her untiring dedication to their foundation, giving a yearly award to those whom she felt contributed significantly to further the cause of medical science. Some of those who received the foundation's cash prize and a reproducton of the *Winged Victory of Samothrace* were Dr. Jonas Salk, developer of the polio vaccine, Dr. Selman Waksman, discoverer of streptomycin and Dr. Henry H. Kessler who made strides in the rehabilitation of the disabled. The awards also began to pique public awareness regarding medical research and ten recipients of the foundation's award went on to win the Nobel Prize.

Along with her extensive work with the foundation, she involved herself in other organizations such as the National Committee for Mental Hygiene where it was her goal to minimize the stigma attached to the issue of mental illness. She has also been associated with the National Health Education Committee, the American Cancer Society, the United Cerebral Palsy Research and Educational Foundation, and the Planned Parenthood Federation.

Mrs. Lasky is also known for her love of beauty and her semi-annual project of planting flowers and greenery around various public buildings in New York City. Through her efforts, the city elders established a "Salute to the Seasons" program in which seasonal plants were used to help beautify the city.

Before her marriage to Albert Lasker, she was married to art dealer Paul Reinhardt for eight years.

LIBERACE (1919-1987), pianist, was born Wladziu Valentino Liberace on May 16, 1919 in West Allis, Wisconsin, son of Salvatore and Frances (Zuchowski) Liberace. He started piano lessons at age four, and when he was seven won a scholarship to the Wisconsin College of Music. During the next seventeen years, he studied there tuition-free. His parents separated during the Depression, and when he was eleven Liberace began to work, playing piano for the silent pictures.

In 1936 he made his first solo appearance with the Chicago Symphony Orchestra, directed by Frederick Stock. However, most of his musical performances as a teenager were with dance bands in Milwaukee area night clubs. In 1940 he went to New York where he played intermission piano for singers at the Plaza Hotel's Persian Room. Exempted from the military draft because of a spinal injury, during World War II Liberace returned to the Milwaukee night clubs and developed a distinctive style for his act. When he went back to the Persian Room after the war, it was with his own "show" piano complete with a Louis XIV candelabrum.

Liberace made his first television appearance in 1951 on a local Los Angeles program, and soon after starred in the *Liberace Show* fifteen minutes every weekday on NBC. By now he had become known for his elaborate costumes (often trimmed with furs, feathers, and jewels) and his flashy showmanship. His repertoire included lavishly embellished versions of current hits, old parlor songs, and widely-known classical pieces. In the early 1950s he was a box office sensation. His performance at Carnegie Hall sold out and he set audience records at Madison Square Garden and the Hollywood Bowl.

In 1956, after William Neil Connor, writing in the London *Daily Mirror* insinuated Liberace might be homosexual, the star's fame plummeted. "I went from the top to the bottom in a very short time, and I had to fight for my life," Liberace recalled later. He sued for libel, and in 1959, won the case. He continued to perform in person and in movies such as *South Seas Sinner* (1950) and *The Loved One* (1959). In 1963 he nearly died of kidney failure after inadvertently inhaling dry-cleaning solvent while cleaning his costumes. This changed his attitude towards performing. He decided to reserve more time for his personal life, by working half as much for twice the money. He began his Las Vegas act, appearing there four to five months of the year until the early 1980s when he decided to tour more.

In between his Las Vegas performances, he appeared on television, wrote the gourmet cookbook, *Liberace Cooks! Recipes from His Seven Dining Rooms* with Carol Truax (1970), and published *The Things I Love* (1976), an illustrated book showing the many lavish possessions in his houses. He also built and promoted the Liberace Museum and Liberace Shopping Plaza in Las Vegas, with the profits going to fund scholarships for young musicians. In 1982, Scott Thorson, once Liberace's employee, sued the pianist for $113 million, saying that Liberace had promised to provide financial support for life in exchange for homosexual favors. The case was dismissed in Los Angeles Superior Court in 1984 with the ruling

that contracts for sexual arrangements are illegal pro-
stitution. On tour during the 1980s, Liberace continued to
be a sensation, playing to a total 82,000 people in fourteen
performances at Radio City Music Hall in 1984, and returning in 1985 and 1986 for sold-out shows. He died on
February 4, 1987 in Palm Springs, California.

LIPPOLD, RICHARD (1915-?) is a well-known artist
whose specialty is sculpting.
 Born in Milwaukee, Wisconsin on May 3, 1915, Lippold studied at the Art Institute of Chicago, graduating
with a B.F.A degree in 1937.
 His first job was with the Chicago Corporation where
he worked as a designer. Three years later, in 1940, he was
an instructor at the Layton School of Art in Milwaukee and
the following year, he worked in the same capacity at the
University of Michigan at Ann Arbor.
 In 1944 Lippold and his wife moved to New York City
and he studied his art, specifically wire sculpting. He
later spent two years teaching at Vermont's Goddard
College.
 In 1947, he held his first one-man show at the
Willard Gallery, and had a second showing there the following year. He continued to be involved in art education,
teaching part time at Queen's College in New York and
overseeing the art department at Trenton Junior College in
New Jersey.
 When he held his third art showing at the Willard
Gallery in 1950, he showed only one sculpture that he titl-
ed *Variation within a Sphere No. 7: Full Moon.* The
Museum of Modern Art acquired the piece and it was a
part of the *Salute to France* show in Paris. That same
year, he was offered a commission to create a sculpture
for the exterior of the Graduate Law School Center at Harvard University. Sculpted in stainless steel, he called it
World Tree.
 Other works of his include: the wire and wood
sculpture *Dead Bird* ; *The Unknown Political Prisoner* ;
Five Variations within a Sphere ; *Variation Number 7:
Full Moon* ; *Aerial Act* ; *Juggler in the Sun* ; *Ganymede* ;
and *The Sun.* The last work was commissioned by the
Metropolitan Museum of Art.
 He uses basic materials such as wire, steel and
plastics and after he was commissioned, along with eight
other sculptors to create a piece of work in silver, he
wrote: "It was evident from the first touching of sterling
silver that it is a most feminine metal...Its extreme

delicacy of surface and precise hardening and softening temperatures, all make it one of the most challenging materials ever worked..."

His other numerous commissions include: the In-land Steel Building, 1958; the Pan Am Building, 1961; Avery Fisher Hall, Lincoln Center, 1961; St. Mary's Cathedral, San Francisco, 1967; Christian Science Center, Boston, 1974; Hyatt Regency, Atlanta, 1975; a 115 foot stainless steel sculpture on the mall in front of the Air and Space Museum in Washington, D.C., 1976; King's Retiring Room, Riyadh, Saudi Arabia, 1977; Shiga Sacred Garden, Kyoto, Japan, 1981; and First Interstate Bank, Seattle, 1985; among others.

His work was also included in the *15 Americans* ex-hibition at the Museum of Modern Art in 1952. An *Art Digest* writer noted that his work "has the constructivist's dynamic equilibrium and depth but it also has purely per-sonal elements of poetry." In a brochure on the *15 Americans* exhibit, Lippold explained his approach to his craft: "My preference in material is Space, captured by the most seductive materials I can arrange. My preference for social action is simply to have my being among all the other objects that exist in Space, 'which loves us all,' and in which modes of communication today can dissolve barriers of time and energy, of nations and races. Although the word sounds old-fashioned, I thus have my faith in Space...Like every adventure, this being in Space at all levels is full of terror, delight, question, and answer."

Lippold is   married to Louise Greuel who studied modern dance with various teachers such as Martha Graham and Merce Cunningham. The couple have three children.

LOOMIS, ORLAND S. (1893-1942), governor-elect, was born on November 2, 1893 in Mauston, Wisconsin, the son of Morgan and Clara (Steen) Loomis. He attended Ripon College and the University of Wisconsin where he receiv-ed a law degree in 1917. He married Florence Ely in 1918. They had three children. That same year, he enlisted in the U.S. Army and was sent to France with a medical sup-ply unit. Returning in 1919, he practiced law in Mauston.

In 1922, Loomis was elected Mauston City Attorney, and   served until   1931. He also served three terms as district attorney of Juneau County. In 1928, he was elected to the State Assembly, where he emerged as a leader of the Progressives. He won election to the Senate in 1930 on the Republican ticket, but in 1934 changed allegiance and joined the newly created Progressive Party. He ran as their candidate for attorney general in 1934, but lost. In 1935, Loomis was appointed director of the state Rural Electrification Authority. He was elected Attorney General in 1935 and served a single term, losing a second election to John C. Martin. Loomis ran as the Progressive candidate for governor in 1940, but was narrowly defeated. He returned two years later to win the governorship, but in December of 1942, before he could enter the office, suffered a series of heart attacks and died. He was forty-nine.

LUCEY, PATRICK J. (1918-), thirty-seventh governor of Wisconsin, was born on March 21, 1918 in La Crosse, Wisconsin, the son of Gregory and Ella (McNamara) Lucey. He attended St. Thomas College from 1936 to 1939, then managed his father's grocery store for three years. In 1941 he joined the army and was sent to the Caribbean. He was discharged in 1945 with the rank of captain. For the following six years, he managed fourteen farms in southwestern Wisconsin. He also returned to school and finished his B.A. at the University of Wisconsin in 1946. In 1951, he married Jean Vlasis. They had three children.

Lucey entered politics in 1948 when he was elected to the State Assembly. Two years later he ran for U.S. Representative, but was defeated. Between 1951 and 1953, he was executive director of the Wisconsin Democratic Party. He later served as chairman of that body. Lucey also worked as a campaign manager. In 1952, he managed Thomas Fairchild's bid for Senate; in 1954, James E. Doyle's race for governor; and in 1957, William Proxmire's run for the U.S. Senate. He was a campaign aide for John F. Kennedy in the 1960 presidential election, and for Robert Kennedy in 1968.

Lucey ran his own successful campaign for lieutenant governor of Wisconsin in 1964. He tried for the governorship two years later, but was defeated by incumbent Warren P. Knowles. He ran again in 1970 and won, becoming the first Wisconsin governor ever elected to a four year term. During his administration, Lucey supported changes to the tax system and the campaign financing law. The legislature passed an ethics code for state officials, and reformed the state revenue sharing system with municipalities. Lucey was reelected to a second term in 1974. He served until July 7, 1977, when he resigned to take an appointment as U.S. Ambassador to Mexico.

LYNCH, THOMAS, (1844-) a U. S. Representative from Wisconsin; born in Granville, Milwaukee County, Wis., November 21, 1844; attended the common schools; moved to Chilton, Calumet County, in 1864; engaged in agricultural pursuits; taught school; held various local offices; member of the State assembly in 1873 and 1883; was graduated from the law department of the Wisconsin University at Madison in 1875; was admitted to the bar in the same year and commenced practice in Chilton, Wis.; district attorney 1878-1882; moved to Antigo, Langlade County, Wis., in 1883; mayor of Antigo in 1885 and 1888; elected as a Democrat to the Fifty-second and Fifty-third Congresses (March 4, 1891-March 3, 1895); died May 4, 1908.

M

MACARTHUR, ARTHUR (1815-1896), Wisconsin's fourth governor, was born in Glasgow, Scotland on January 26, 1815, the son of Arthur and Sarah (MacArthur) MacArthur. His father died when he was very young, and his mother brought him to the United States. MacArthur attended Wesleyan University in Middletown, Connecticut, and then studied law in New York City. He was admitted to the New York Bar in 1840. He practiced law for a short time in New York, then moved to Massachusetts, and in 1843 became Public Administrator for Hampden County. He also served as judge for the Western Massachusetts Military District.

MacArthur married Aurelia Blecher about 1845, and they had one son, Arthur MacArthur, who later became Military Governor of the Philippines. In 1849, MacArthur moved his family to Milwaukee where he set up a law practice. He was appointed City Attorney in 1851. Four years later he ran as the Democratic candidate for lieutenant governor in an election with incumbent Governor Barstow. MacArthur won easily, but Barstow was reelected by only a narrow margin and resigned shortly after his inauguration. There was dispute as to whether Barstow had actually won the governorship over Republican challenger, Coles Bashford. Upon Barstow's resignation, MacArthur, as lieutenant governor, felt obligated to take over the office. But within a few days, Bashford informed MacArthur that he was assuming the governorship, peacefully if possible, but by force if necessary. MacArthur yielded in order to avert violence, and returned to preside over the State Senate as lieutenant governor. His term as governor had lasted four days.

In 1857, MacArthur was elected Judge of the Second Circuit, a post he held until 1869. He served as United States commissioner to the Paris Exposition in 1867. In 1868, his wife, Aurelia, died, and in 1871 he married Mary E. (Wilcut) Hopkins. In 1870, President Grant appointed MacArthur to the Supreme Court of the District of Columbia. MacArthur retired in 1888 and remained in Washington, D.C. until his death on August 26, 1896.

MARQUETTE, JACQUES, (1637-1675), missionary and explorer, was born in Laon, France, in 1637. He entered the Society of Jesus in 1654, and was ordained a priest twelve years later. Going to Canada in 1666, he arrived in Quebec on September 20th, and soon afterward proceeded to the country of the Algonquin and Huron tribes, where he spent eighteen months studying their languages. In the spring of 1668 he went with a party of Nez-Perces to Lake Superior, and renewed the abandoned mission which had been established there as early as 1641 by the Jesuit fathers Raymbault and Jacques. It was called Sault Sainte Marie, and was the first permanent settlement in Michigan.

After building a church there and converting many Indians, Marquette went to La Pointe du St. Esprit, and in 1671 he founded the mission of St. Ignatius at Mackinaw. Two years later in pursuance of orders issued by Frontenac, Governor of Canada, Marquette joined Louis Jolliet on an exploring expedition, a record of which he preserved in a journal, which, aside from its charming style and beautiful descriptions, discloses remarkable powers of observation and scientific insight into natural phenomena. He was the first to offer an explanation of the lake tides, and his theory has not been changed by modern scientists.

In October, 1674, Father Marquette was commanded to establish a mission in Illinois, and although his health had been shattered by the recent hardships, he traveled along the western shore of Lake Michigan, proceeding as far as the Chicago River. He was too exhausted to proceed farther, but during the winter he sufficiently recovered during to resume the journey the following March, and he reached Kaskasia April 8, 1675. He remained there for a while, preaching the gospel, and converting several thousand Indian men and women. Obliged by his illness to leave Kaskasia, he set out for Mackinaw, escorted by the Indians, but his health was rapidly failing, and he did not reach his destination. He died near Marquette River, Michigan, May 18, 1675. The remains were transferred to Point St. Ignace, Michigan, and their burial place was forgotten until discovered by a clergyman of Eagle Harbor, Michigan, in 1877. Father Marquette's journal entitled *Voyage et decouverte de quelques pays et nations de l'Amerique Septentrionale*, is translated in J. G. Shea's *Discovery and Exploration of the Mississippi* (1852).

MCCARTHY, JOSEPH R. (1909-1957), U.S. senator, was born November 14, 1909 in Grand Chute, Wisconsin, the son of Timothy and Bridget (Tierney) McCarthy. As a boy, he went to Underhill country school and worked on his father's farm. He attended Marquette University and received his LL.B. degree in 1935. McCarthy practiced law for several years and at age twenty-nine was elected the youngest circuit judge in Wisconsin's history.

During World War II, McCarthy served as a ground officer for Marine Air Force Intelligence in the Pacific, rose to the rank of captain, and won several citations. He returned to Wisconsin in 1945 and was re-elected circuit judge. The following year, he ran for U.S. Senate against incumbent Robert La Follette, whose family had held a Senate seat for the past forty years, and won the Republican nomination. He was elected to the Senate that November, and re-elected in 1952.

While in the Senate, McCarthy gained an international reputation as an ardent anti-Communist. In a speech in Wheeling, West Virginia in February 1950, he stirred controversy by accusing the State Department of hiring Communists. As chairman of the Senate Government Operations Committee and its subcommittee on investigations, he conducted zealous hearings to root out alleged Communist sympathizers in the government and the entertainment industry. His critics charged him with character assasination and political opportunism. With the blacklist, fear, and censorship as its tools, McCarthyism swept the nation, ruining many lives and careers in Washington, New York, and Hollywood. McCarthy's strident tactics came into public view in 1954 when for 36 days his hearings into alleged communism in the Army were televised. In the ensuing furor, the Senate voted to censure McCarthy for his "conduct toward the Senate and the Arthur V. Watkins special committee" on December 1, 1954. McCarthy died in Bethesda, Maryland on May 2, 1957.

MCCORD, MYRON HOWLER, (1840-1908) a U. S. Representative from Wisconsin; born in Ceres, McKean County, Pa., November 26, 1840; attended Richburg Academy, New York; moved to Wisconsin in 1854 and settled in Shawano, Shawano County; moved to Merrill in 1875; became a publisher, lumberman, and farmer; published a newspaper 1868-1883; served in the State senate in 1873 and 1874; member of the State assembly in 1881; delegate to the Republican National Convention in 1876; register of the United States land office at Wausau, Wis., from February 26, 1884, to June 24, 1885; elected as a Republican to the Fifty-first Congress (March 4, 1889-March 3, 1891); unsuccessful candidate for reelection in 1890 to the Fifty-second Congress and for election in 1892 to the Fiftythird Congress; returned to Merrill, Wis., and engaged in agricultural pursuits and lumbering; appointed by President McKinley as Governor of Arizona Territory in 1897; resigned in 1898 and organized the Territorial Regiment for the Spanish-American War; appointed United States marshal for the district of Arizona May 1, 1902, and served until July 1, 1905; later appointed collector of customs for the port of Nogales, Ariz.; died in Phoenix, Ariz., on April 27, 1908; interment in Merrill Cemetery, Merrill, Lincoln County, Wis.

MCDILL, ALEXANDER STUART, (1822-1875) a U. S. Representative from Wisconsin; born near Meadville, Crawford County, Pa., on March 18, 1822; attended Allegheny College; was graduated from Cleveland Medical College in 1848 and practiced medicine in Crawford County, Pa., 1848-1856; moved to Plover, Portage County, Wis., in 1856; member of the State assembly in 1862; member of the board of managers of the Wisconsin State Hospital for the Insane 1862-1868; served in the State senate in 1863 and 1864; medical superintendent of the Wisconsin State Hospital for the Insane 1868-1873 and in 1875; elected as a Republican to the Forty-third Congress (March 4, 1873-March 3, 1875); unsuccessful candidate for reelection to the Forty-fourth Congress; died near Madison, Wis., November 12, 1875; interment in Forest Hill Cemetery, Madison, Wis.

MEMURRAY, HOWARD JOHNSTONE, (1901-1961) a U. S. Representative from Wisconsin; born in Harvey County, near Mount Hope, Kans., March 3, 1901; attended the public schools, Berea Academy at Berea, Ky., and high school at Madison, Wis.; was graduated from the University of Wisconsin at Madison in 1936; engaged in the life insurance business 1923-1928; executive with air transport companies 1928-1935; teacher of political science at the University of Wisconsin 1936-1942; elected as a Democrat to the Seventy-eighth Congress (January 3, 1943-January 3, 1945); was not a candidate for renomination in 1944, but was an unsuccessful Democratic candidate for election to the United States Senate in 1944 and again in 1946; lecturer in political science at the University of Wisconsin in 1945 and 1946; professor of political science at Occidental College, Los Angeles, Calif., 1947-1949; professor of government, University of New Mexico, from 1949 until his death in Albuquerque, N.Mex., August 14, 1961; interment in Fairview Park Cemetery.

MINOR, EDWARD SLOMAN, (1840-1924) a U. S. Representative from Wisconsin; born at Point Peninsula, Jefferson County, N.Y., December 13, 1840; moved to Wisconsin in 1845 with his parents, who settled in Greenfield, Milwaukee County, and subsequently in the city of Milwaukee; attended the common schools; went with his parents to a farm in Sheboygan County in 1852 and engaged in agricultural pursuits; completed a common-school education; enlisted as a private in Company G, Second Regiment, Wisconsin Volunteer Cavalry, in 1861; mustered out as first lieutenant in November 1865; engaged in the hardware business in Sturgeon Bay, Wis., 1865-1884; member of the Wisconsin assembly in 1877, 1881, and 18S2; served in the State senate 1883-1886 and as president pro tempore of the senate during the last term; superintendent of the Sturgeon Bay and Lake Michigan Ship Canal 1884-1891; member of the Wisconsin Fish Commission for four years; mayor of Sturgeon Bay in 1894; elected as a Republican to the Fifty-fourth and to the five succeeding Congresses (March 4, 1895-March 3, 1907); chairman, Committee on Expenditures in the Department of the Interior (Fifty-eighth and Fifty-ninth Congresses); unsuccessful candidate for renomination in 1906; engaged in horticulture; postmaster of Sturgeon Bay 1911-1915; again mayor of Sturgeon Bay in 1918; died at Sturgeon Bay, Wis., July 26, 1924; interment in Bayside Cemetery.

MONAHAN, JAMES GIDEON, (1855-1923) a U. S. Representative from Wisconsin; born at Willow Springs, near Darlington, Lafayette County, Wis., January 12, 1855; attended the common schools and was graduated from the Darlington High School in 1875; taught school; studied law; was admitted to the bar in 187S and commenced practice in Mineral Point, Wis.; returned to Darlington in 1880; district attorney of Lafayette County 1880-1884; editor and owner of the Darlington Republican Journal 1883-1919; delegate to the Republican National Convention in 1888; collector of internal revenue for the second Wisconsin district 1900-1908; elected as a Republican to the Sixty-sixth Congress (March 4, 1919-March 3, 1921); unsuccessful candidate for renomination in 1920 to the Sixty-seventh Congress; died in Dubuque, Iowa, December 5, 1923; interment in Union Grove Cemetery, Darlington, Wis.

MOODY, JIM, (1935-1925) a U. S. Representative from Wisconsin; born James Powers Moody in Richlands, Tazewell County, Va., September 2, 1935; B.A., Haverford College, Haverford, Pa., 1957; M.P.A., Harvard University, 1967; Ph.D., University of California, Berkeley, 1973; Peace Corps and CARE assignments in Yugoslavia, Iran, and Pakistan, 1958-1965; econo-mist for Federal Government, 1967-1969; elected, Wisconsin assembly, 1977-1978; elected, Wisconsin senate, 1979-1982; delegate, Wisconsin State Democratic conventions, 1977 1982; elected as a Democrat to the Ninety-eighth and to the two succeeeding Congresses (January 3, 1983-January 3, 1989); is a resident of Milwaukee, Wis. MOODY, Malcolm Adelbert, a U. S. Representative from Oregon; born in Linn County, near the present town of Brownsville, Oreg., November 30, 1854; moved with his parents to Illinois the next year and to The Dalles, Wasco County, Oreg., in 1862; attended the public schools and the University of California at Berkeley; engaged in mercantile pursuits at The Dalles, Oreg .; cashier of The Dalles National Bank; member of the city council 1885-1889; elected mayor of The Dalles in 1889 and server two terms; member of the Republican State central and congressional committees from 1888 to 1898; elected as a Republican to the Fifty-sixth and Fifty-seventh Congresses (March 4, 1899-March 3, 1903); was not a candidate for renomination in 1902 to the Fifty-eighth Congress; resumed the mercantile business at The Dalles, Oreg.; died in Portland, Oreg., on March 19, 1925; interment in Odd Fellows Cemetery, The Dalles, Oreg.

MOOREHEAD, AGNES (1906-1974), actress, was born in Clinton, Massachusetts on December 6, 1906, the daughter of John and Mary (McCauley) Moorehead. Her family moved to Wisconsin while she was young, and Moorehead received her early education in Reedsburg. She attended Muskingum College in Ohio and did graduate work in English and public speaking at the University of Wisconsin. After graduation, she took a position in Soldiers Grove, Wisconsin as a teacher of English and public speaking. She also served as drama director for the town.

In 1923, Moorehead made her first performance on radio, then a new medium, singing on stations KMOX and KSO in St. Louis. She also performed as a singer and dancer with the St. Louis Municipal Opera Company for three seasons in its annual festivals. Soon after, she moved to New York to train for the stage at the American Academy of Dramatic Arts. She appeared in a number of Broadway productions; however, with the Depression, the opportunity for theater work declined. She turned to radio, and appeared in the comedies *Cavalcade of America* and *The March of Time,* and a daytime serial.

During this time she joined the Mercury Players and met Orson Welles, who directed the company. In 1941, he chose her for the part of Kane's mother in the movie, *Citizen Kane.* This small but memorable role brought her into the public view. She starred in more of Welles' pictures, among them *The Magnificent Ambersons* (1942) in which she played a neurotic aunt, a part that won her the New York Film Critics' Award and a nomination from the Academy of Motion Pictures Arts and Sciences. In the course of her career, she received five Academy Award nominations and she appeared in more than a hundred motion pictures, among them, *Johnny Belinda* (1948) and *Hush...Hush, Sweet Charlotte* (1965). She returned to the stage and appeared in many Broadway productions, most notably, *Don Juan in Hell* (1951, 1973) and *Gigi* (1973). She also enchanted the general public as Endora in the 1960s television series *Bewitched.* Agnes Moorehead died on April 30, 1974.

MUIR, JOHN, (1838-1914), geologist, naturalist and author, was born in Dunbar, Haddingtonshire, Scotland, April 21, 1838, third child of Daniel and Anne (Gilrye) Muir. Daniel Muir, a grain merchant, was able to give his eight children a good education—John's, which extended over a period of eight years, comprising the ordinary English branches, Latin, French, the Catechism and the Bible. In 1849 the family emigrated to the United States, and settled near Fox River, Wisconsin. About twelve miles from Fort Winnebago, they cleared a tract of wild land for a farm. John Muir did his full share of the manual labor involved in subduing the forest. At the same time he read every book within reach and studied mathematics, keeping his books by him in the field and working out problems on the ground or on chips from the trees he had fallen. He had a decided taste for mechanics, and was called a great genius by his neighbors. The young man was accustomed to rise soon after midnight to make wooden clocks, millwheels and other appliances of his own invention.

John Muir entered the University of Wisconsin at the age of twenty-two, and completed the four years' course, paying his way with money earned by harvesting and by school-teaching. Then he vanished in the grand American wildernesses, coming in sight from time to time on farms and in mills and factories, when his bread-money gave out. His first botanical and geological excursions were made in

Wisconsin, Indiana, Michigan and Canada, around the Great Lakes; the next through the southern states. In search of rare plants he penetrated the swamps of Florida, camping out without cover of any sort, and consequently contracted malaria, which prevented him from going on to South America, to explore the head-waters of the Amazon, as he had planned.

After partially recovering, Muir spent a month in Cuba and then crossed the Isthmus of Panama and proceeded to California, where he arrived in April, 1868. He visited the Yosemite Valley for the purpose of examining its flora and finally was allowed to make the valley his home, being put in charge of a mill there, which he built to saw fallen pines. He earned enough to support himself for a long time, his habits being frugal, and now began a systematic exploration of the mountain region in which the great valley is situated. Emerson, whom he guided through the Yosemite, said of him: "He is more wonderful than Thoreau."

For ten years Muir led an isolated life in the Sierra Nevada, undergoing hardships and often subjected to great dangers. Only when his stock of bread ran out did he return to civilization. His winters were devoted to study and to elaborating his notes. The flora and fauna and the meteorology of that region were minutely studied, but his work as a geologist was far more important. The effects of the glacial period constituted the main subject of his investigation for many years, and he discovered sixty-five small residual glaciers on the High Sierra. His first article on these glaciers appeared in the New York *Tribune* in 1871.

Muir was offered many inducements to prepare himself for professorships in colleges, but declined them, declaring that he wanted "to be more than a professor, whether noticed in the world or not, and that there were already far too many professors as compared with students in the field." From 1876 to 1878, he was a member of an exploring party connected with the geodetic survey in the Great Basin. Muir next made several trips to Oregon, Washington and Alaska. He made his first trip to Alaska was made in 1879, the year in which he discovered what is now called Glacier Bay and the enormous glacier that bears his name. He also reached the waters of Yukon and the MacKenzie. In 1881, he pushed still farther north, being connected with one of the search expeditions for the lost Jeannette expedition.

He published only the book, *The Mountains of California* in 1894. "This book," said the New York *Witness* "should take high rank among the productions of American naturalists for the information which it contains; and yet it reads like a novel." The San Francisco *Call* declared that, "no man since Thoreau ever had keener sympathy with nature, a quicker vision for her mysteries, or a surer speech for their interpretation than Mr. Muir." Muir's publications, about 150 in number in 1897, were chiefly in the form of articles contributed to the *Overland Monthly*, *Harper's*, the *Century*, the San Francisco *Bulletin*, and other magazines and newspapers. In them he described the magnificent scenery of the west side of the continent, its mountain ranges, glaciers, forests, rivers, wild gardens, animals, etc. Among these articles were: "On the Formation of Mountians in the Sierra"; "On the Post-Glacial History of Sequoia Gigantes"; "Glaciation of Arctic and Sub-Arctic Regions"; "Alaska Glaciers"; "Alaska Rivers"; "Ancient Glaciers of the Sierra"; "Forests of Alaska"; "Orgin of Yosemite Valley"; "American Forests"; "Forest Reservations and National Parks".

As a forest wanderer Muir was a friend of trees, and for twenty years or more made a call to "Save the forests!" The establishment of the Yosemite and Sequoia national parks and the great Sierra Forest Reservation was brought about by his writings, and the work of his forest-loving friends; especially R. U. Johnson, of the *Century Magazine*. He was the editor of *Picturesque California*, and the author of most of the text describing mountain scenery.

In 1879 Muir was married to the daughter of Dr. John Strentzel, of California, and after that time gave attention to the management of fine fruit ranch, inherited by his wife; but he never allowed it to stand in the way of his scientific pursuits. In 1896, the honorary degree of A.M. was conferred on him by Harvard University, and the following year that of LL.D. by the Wisconsin State University. John Muir died in 1914.

MURRAY, REID FRED, (1887-1952) a U. S. Representative from Wisconsin; born in Ogdensburg, Waupaca County, Wis., October 16, 1887; attended the public schools and Manawa High School; was graduated from the College of Agriculture of the University of Wisconsin at Madison in 1916; served as agricultural agent for railroads in St. Paul, Minn., 1914-1917, for Winnebago County, Wis.,

117-1919, and for the First National Bank, Oshkosh, Wis., 1919-1922; professor of animal husbandry, at the College of Agriculture, University of Wisconsin, 1922-1927; engaged in agricultural pursuits and in the buying and selling of cattle and farms, Waupaca, Wis., 1927-1939; elected as a Republican to the Seventy-sixth and to the six succeeding Congresses and served from January 3, 1939, until his death in Bethesda, Md., April 29, 1952; interment in Park Cemetery, one mile north of Ogdensburg, Wis.

N

NELSON, GAYLORD ANTON (1916-   ), thirty-fourth governor of Wisconsin, was born on June 4, 1916 in Clear Lake, Wisconsin, the son of Anton and Mary (Bradt Hogan) Nelson. After receiving his education at San Jose State College in California, and the University of Wisconsin Law School, he was admitted to the Wisconsin Bar in 1942. During World War II, he served in the U.S. Army in the Pacific Theater. In 1946 he returned and began a law practice in Madison. He ran as a Republican for the Wisconsin State Assembly that same year, but lost the election. In 1947, he married Carrie Lee Dotson. They had three children.

Nelson changed his affiliation to the Democratic Party in 1948, and ran for the State Senate. He served for three consecutive terms, until 1958. During that time, in 1954, he ran for the U.S. House of Representatives, but lost to Glenn R. Davis. Nelson ran for the governorship of Wisconsin in 1958, and was elected, becoming the first Democratic governor since 1932. He served for two terms. During his administration, Nelson reorganized the state government, creating a Department of Economic Development, Department of Administration, and a State Commission on Aging. He supported conservation efforts with the passage of the Outdoor Recreation Act of 1961.

Nelson decided not to run for a third term as governor. In 1964, he ran for a seat in the U.S. Senate and won. He has remained in the Senate since then, serving on numerous committees including the Finance Committee, the Select Committee on Small Business, the Subcommittee on Private Pension Plans, the Subcommittee on Monopoly, and the Subcommittee on Employment, Poverty, and Migratory Labor.

NIEMAN, LUCIUS WILLIAM, (1857-1935), newspaper publisher, was born at Bear Creek, Wisconsin, December 13, 1857, son of Conrad and Sara Elizabeth (Delamatter) Nieman. Orphaned at an early age, he was reared by his maternal grandmother. In 1870, after a limited public school education, he began his career in journalism as a printer's apprentice in the composing room of the Waukesha, Wisconsin *Freeman*. Later he went in a similar capacity to the Milwaukee *Sentinel*, interrupting his employment there to attend Carroll College in Waukesha from 1875-76.

When he returned to the *Sentinel* in 1876 he was soon made a reporter, then, in swift succession: legislative coorespondent in Madison, the state capital; city editor; and managing editor, before he was twenty-one. The *Sentinel* was then the largest newspaper in Wisconsin, and as its managing editor Nieman won recognition as one of the ablest journalists in the state. Later he spent a year in St. Paul, Minnesota, as editor and part owner of the St. Paul *Dispatch*, a decadent newspaper which he transformed into a revitalized and prosperous property. He then returned to Milwaukee as managing editor of the *Sentinel*.

In the fall of 1882, Nieman and Michael Kraus purchased the mechanical equipment of a political campaign paper which had been started a few weeks earlier and established the *Daily Journal* (later the *Milwaukee Journal*) as an afternoon newspaper. The initial issue was published, November 16, 1882, with Nieman as its editor, a position he held until his death. The business was incorporated, February 5, 1883, under the name of the *Journal Co.*, with a capital stock of $15,000, the two owners subscribing equal amounts. The capital stock was increased to $20,000 in June of 1890, Nieman securing the majority interest which he held for the rest of his life.

From the outset the *Journal* crusaded against special interests and corrupt politics and for strict regulation of public utilities, equitable distribution of the tax burden, conservation of the state's natural resources, reforestation of waste lands, creation of state parks, building of better highways and other measures of public welfare. In 1890 it conducted a spectacular fight against the Bennett Law, which required that instruction be given in English in private and parochial, as well as public, schools throughout the state. The *Journal* also campaigned for eight years against the practice of permitting state treasurers to appropriate to their own use the interest paid on deposits of state funds, finally bringing about court action that resulted in the restitution to the State Treasury of some $500,000 which had been misapplied.

During World War I, despite the preponderance of the German element in the population of Wisconsin, the *Journal* gave unreserved support to the cause of the United States and its allies, waging a vigorous campaign against pro-Germanism and all antagonism to the aims of the American government. As a result it was awarded the Pulitzer Prize in 1919 for "the most disinterested and meritorious service rendered by any American newspaper during 1918."

In taking over the *Journal* in 1882, Nieman announced that it would be an "independent organ of the people," free from political dictation and control. While it more frequently supported Democratic policies and candidates than those of the Republican Party, its course was always determined by Nieman's earnest convictions as to the merits of the candidates and the policies for which they stood. Under his leadership the *Journal* became the largest, most influential and prosperous newspaper in Wisconsin, with an average week-day circulation of 185,000, a Sunday edition of 225,000 copies and a publishing plant unexcelled in equipment and service facilities by any other newspaper in a city of comparable size in the country.

While he continued as its president and editor until his death, he progressively relinquished active management of the paper during the last decagde of his life, devoting much of his time to travel. He was married in Milwaukee, November 28, 1900, to Agnes Elizabeth Guenther. Mrs. Nieman, who did not long survive him, bequeathed to Harvard University the Lucius W. Nieman and Agnes Wahl Nieman Fund, a trust fund amounting to approximately $1,000,000 for the establishment and maintenance of a group of fellowships, starting with eight and awarded to working newspapermen "to promote and elevate the standards of journalism in the United States." Nieman died in Milwaukee, Wisconsin, October 1, 1935.

O

OBEY, DAVID BOSS, (1938-) a U. S. Representative from Wisconsin; born in Okmulgee, Okmulgee County, Okla., October 3, 1938; graduated from Wausau High School, 1956; M.A. degree in political science, University of Wisconsin, 1960; elected to the Wisconsin State assembly in 1962 and reelected in 1964, 1966 and 1968; licensed real estate broker; elected as a Democrat to the Ninety-first Congress, by special election, April 1, 1969, to fill the vacancy caused by the resignation of Melvin R. Laird; reelected to the nine succeeding Congresses (April 1, 1969, to January 3, 1989); chairman, Joint Economic Committee (Ninety-ninth Congress); is a resident of Wausau, Wis.

O'KEEFFE, GEORGIA (1887-1986), painter, was born November 15, 1887 in Sun Prairie, Wisconsin, but left the State early in her career. Her reputation was founded on a series of brilliant close-ups of flowers and arrangements of exotic objects and scenes, among which the seashore, the New Mexico desert, bleached animal skulls, and New York skyscrapers were favorite themes. Her work contained a marked element of abstraction, and the shapes and colors of her compositions expressed strong emotion.

By the time she was twelve, O'Keeffe had decided she wanted to be a painter. She enrolled in the Art Institute of Chicago in 1904 and studied for a year with John Vanderpoel. From 1907 to 1908 she studied at the Art Students League in New York, under Francis Luis Mora and William Merritt Chase, then went back to Chicago and worked as a freelance artist a few years. From 1912 to 1916, O'Keeffe worked as the supervisor of art in Amarillo, Texas public schools. During the summers she taught summer school at the University of Virginia. She also taught in South Carolina at Columbia College. In 1915 she spent the summer in New York at Teachers College, Columbia University, studying art under Alon Bement and Arthur Dow. Her art, which she had laid aside while teaching,

99

now took on a new interest for her. She returned to Texas to head the art department at West Texas State Normal College, and to paint and draw.

About this time, at her request, O'Keeffe's friend, Anita Pollitzer, took a roll of Georgia's charcoal drawings to Alfred Stieglitz, the photographer and New York modern art exhibitor. Without O'Keeffe's knowledge, Stieglitz showed the drawings at his next opening at the "291" Gallery on Fifth Avenue. Although the unauthorized display displeased O'Keeffe, it was responsible for making her known as an artist and for opening her works to the professional critics (many of whose comments bothered her.) Stieglitz encouraged O'Keeffe to continue with her art, and in 1918 she moved to New York and pursued her painting as part of the Stieglitz circle.

O'Keeffe's work became well-known and her intense style was so recognizable that in her first major show, "One Hundred Pictures," at the Anderson Galleries in 1923, her paintings were hung unsigned. On December 11, 1924, she and Stieglitz were married. She continued painting, and her work was so prolific that Stieglitz presented her art in one-man shows once a year until 1946. Other exhibitions of her work were held at the Brooklyn Museum of Art (1927); the Art Institute of Chicago (1943); Museum of Modern Art, New York (1946); Dallas Museum of Fine Arts (1953); and Worcester Art Museum (1960).

After her husband died in 1945, O'Keeffe moved to New Mexico and bought an adobe house outside of Abiquiu where she could paint and garden with a view of the mountains. She lived there the rest of her life, leaving only to travel—one of her great loves. Her trips included a three month round-the-world tour in 1959, visits to the Middle East, the Far East, Greece, as well as vacation trips to nearby states. She once said: "The painting is like a thread that runs through all the reasons for all the other things that make one's life." She died in Santa Fe, March 6, 1986 at the age of 98.

O'KONSKI, ALVIN EDWARD, (1904-1987) a U. S. Representative from Wisconsin; born on a farm near Kewaunee, Kewaunee County, Wis., May 26, 1904; attended the public schools and the University of Iowa at Iowa City; was graduated from State Teachers College, Oshkosh, Wis., in 1927, and from the University of Wisconsin at Madison in 1932; instructor in high schools at Omro and Oconto, Wis., 1926-1929; member of the faculty of Oregon State College at Corvallis 1929-1931, and at the University of Detroit,

Detroit, Mich., 1936-1938; superintendent of schools, Pulaski, Wis., 1932-1935; instructor at a junior college, Coleraine, Minn., in 1936; educator, journalist, and lecturer; editor and publisher, Hurler, Wis., 1940-1942; elected as a Republican to the Seventy-eighth and to the fourteen succeeding Congresses (January 3, 1943-January 3, 1973); unsuccessful candidate for nomination in 1957 to the United States Senate to fill a vacancy; unsuccessful candidate for reelection in 1972 to the Ninety-third Congress; was a resident of Rhinelander, Wis., until his death in Kewaunee, Wis., on July 8, 1987; interment in St. Hedwig's Cemetery.

O'MALLEY, THOMAS DAVID PATRICK, (1903-1979) a U. S. Representative from Wisconsin; born in Milwaukee, Wis., March 24, 1903; attended the parochial schools; was graduated from Loyola Academy in 1920, after which he attended Loyola College, and the Y.M.C.A. College of Liberal Arts, Chicago, Ill.; engaged as a salesman, advertising writer, and as an author; delegate to the Democratic National Convention in 1932; unsuccessful candidate for election in 1928 to the Seventy-first Congress and in 1930 to the Seventy-second Congress; elected as a Democrat to the Seventy-third, Seventy-fourth, and Seventy-fifth Congresses (March 4, 1933-January 3, 1939); unsuccessful candidate for reelection in 1938 to the Seventy-sixth Congress; member of the Democratic national congressional committee 1933-1939; resumed advertising and public relations work; regional director of Wage and Hour and Public Contracts Division, United States Department of Labor, Chicago, Ill., 1939-1956; engaged in public relations and management counseling; was a resident of Chicago, Ill., until his death there on December 19, 1979; interment in Neenah, Wis.

OSHKOSH (1795-1850), Menominee Indian head chief, served in that position during the second quarter of the 19th century in Wisconsin. Oshkosh, who earned his reputation as a brave warrior under Tomah and Tecumseh, was the grandson of Cha-kau-cho-ka-ma (Indian for "Old King"). He went to war at the age of seventeen to fight with the British army against the Americans during in War of 1812. With one hundred other Menominee, Oshkosh joined Colonel Robert Kickson in taking Fort Mackinaw in Michigan in 1812. The following year, however, he was a member of the force that was repelled in its attack on Fort Sandusky in Ohio.

On August 11, 1827, Oshkosh was recognized by the United States as the head chief of the Menominee Tribe. The Treaty of Butte des Morts, Wisconsin was the legal document that called him chief even though the U.S. Indian commissioners had already appointed him to be the Menominee spokesman. Although he was intelligent, courageous, and able, Oshkosh had a weakness for alcohol. Once, while under the influence, he murdered an innocent fellow Indian who had done nothing to provoke him.

Oshkosh died in 1850. He was buried in Kenesha, but his remains were moved in 1927 to Menominee Park in the city of Oshkosh.

P

PEAVEY, HUBERT HASKELL, (1881-1937) a U. S. Representative from Wisconsin; born in Adams, Mower County, Minn., on January 12, 1881; moved with his parents to Redwood Falls, Minn., in 1886; attended the public schools, the high school at Redwood Falls, and Pillsbury Academy, Owatonna, Minn.; pursued various activities in Nebraska, Kansas, and Oklahoma from 1900 until 1904, when he moved to South Dakota and engaged in the real estate business; moved to Washburn, Bayfield County, Wis., in 1909 and continued the real estate business; served as alderman in 1911 and as mayor of Washburn in 1912 and 1920-1922; member of the State assembly 1913-1915; became editor and publisher of the Washburn News in 1915; during the First World War recruited Company D, Sixth Infantry, Wisconsin National Guard, and served as captain; resumed his former newspaper activities in Washburn, Wis.; unsuccessful candidate for the Republican nomination in 1920 to the Sixty-seventh Congress; elected as a Republican to the Sixty-eighth and to the five succeeding Congresses (March 4, 1923-January 3, 1935); unsuccessful candidate for reelection in 1934 to the Seventy-fourth Congress; again engaged in the real estate business and also operated a fur ranch; died in Washburn, Wis., November 21, 1937; interment in Woodland Cemetery.

PHILIPP, EMANUEL L. (1861-1925), Wisconsin's twenty-third governor, was born near Honey Creek, Wisconsin on March 25, 1861, the son of Luzi and Sabina (Ludwig) Philipp. After completing high school, he became a telegrapher and agent for the Chicago and Northwestern Railroad. In the years that followed he worked as a train dispatcher and a contracting freight agent. He married Bertha Schweke in 1887. They had three children.

Between 1889 and 1897, Philipp worked as: a general agent for the Gould lines including the American Refrigerator Transit Company, traffic manager of the Schlitz Brewery, and manager of a lumber company. He became president of the American Refrigerator Transit

Company of St. Louis in 1897, and six years later he bought the organization and moved it to Wisconsin.

Philipp became active in Republican politics about 1900 when he served as chairman of the Milwaukee County Convention. At one time a supporter of La Follette, Philipp broke with him in 1904 and published *The Truth About Wisconsin Freight Rates*, a paper refuting La Follette's stance on the issue. Philipp served as police commissioner of Milwaukee from 1909 to 1914. In 1914, he ran for governor, and won. He was elected to two subsequent terms in 1916 and 1918. Philipp's administration was marked by state contributions to the war effort in World War I and aid to returning veterans. The State Legislature passed the Prohibition Enforcement Act in 1919 to conform to federal law.

Philipp returned to his businesses after three terms as governor. He was a regent of Marquette University and also supported efforts of the Wisconsin Humane Society. He died on June 15, 1925.

POUND, THADDEUS COLEMAN, (1833-1914) a U. S. Representative from Wisconsin; born in Elk, Warren County, Pa., December 6, 1833; moved with his parents to Monroe County, N.Y., in 1838; later moved to Rochester, N.Y.; attended the common schools, Milton (Wis.) Academy, and Rushford Academy, Allegany County, N.Y.; moved to Rock County, Wis., in May 1856; engaged in the manufacture of lumber; president of the Union Lumbering Co. and of the Chippewa Falls & Western Railway Co.; member of the State assembly in 1864, 1866, 1867, and 1869, and served the last year as speaker pro tempore; Lieutenant Governor of Wisconsin in 1870 and 1871; delegate to the Republican National Convention in 1872; elected as a Republican to the Forty-fifth, Forty-sixth, and Forty-seventh Congresses (March 4, 1877-March 3, 1883); chairman, Committee on Public Lands (Forty-seventh Congress); was not a candidate for renomination in 1882 to the Forty-eighth Congress; president of the Chippewa Spring Water Co.; died in a hospital in Chicago, Ill., on November 21, 1914; interment in Forest Hill Cemetery, Chippewa Falls, Wis.

PRICE, WILLIAM THOMPSON (FATHER OF HUGH HIRAM PRICE), (a U. S. Representative from Wisconsin; born in Huntingdon County, Pa., June 17, 1824; attended the common schools; was a clerk in a store in Hollidaysburg, Pa., and also studied law; moved to Mount Pleasant, Iowa, in 1845, and in the following autumn moved to Black River Falls, Wis.; engaged in lumbering and agricultrual pursuits; deputy sheriff of Crawford County in 1849; member of the Wisconsin State assembly in 1851 and again in 1882; was admitted to the bar in 1852 and engaged in the practice of law; in 1854 moved to La Crosse, Wis., and operated a stage line between La Crosse and Black River Falls; moved to Black River Falls and continued the practice of law until 1857; judge of Jackson County in 1854 and 1859; under sheriff of Crawford County in 1855; county treasurer in 1856 and 1857; served in the State senate in 1857, 1870, and 1S78-1881, and was president of the Senate in 1879; collector of internal revenue 1863-1865; elected as a Republican to the Forty-eighth and Forty-ninth Congresses and served from March 4, 1883, until his death at Black River Falls, Jackson County, Wis., December 6, 1886; interment in Riverside Cemetery.

PROXMIRE, WILLIAM, (1915-) a U. S. Senator from Wisconsin; born in Lake Forest, Lake County, Ill., November 11, 1915; attended the public schools of Lake Forest and the Hill School, Pottstown, Pa.; graduated, Yale University 1938, Harvard Business School 1 940, and Harvard Graduate School of Arts and Sciences 1948; during the Second World War served in the Military Intelligence Service 1941-1946, member, Wisconsin State assembly 1951-1952; businessman; unsuccessful Democratic candidate for Governor of Wisconsin in 1952, 1954, and 1956 ; elected as a Democrat to the United States Senate in 1957 to fill the vacancy caused by the death of Joseph R. McCarthy and served from August 28, 1957, to January 3, 1959; reelected in 1959, 1964, 1970, 1976, and again in 1982 for the term ending Jaunary 3, 1989; chairman, Committee on Banking, Housing, and Urban Affairs (Ninety-fourth, Ninety-fifth, Ninety-sixth, and One-hundreth Congresses).

Q

QUARLES, JOSEPH VERY, (1843-1911) a U. S. Senator from Wisconsin; born in Southport (now Kenosha), Kenosha County, Wis., December 16, 1843; attended the common schools and the University of Michigan at Ann Arbor; during the Civil War served in the Union Army in the Thirty-ninth Regiment, Wisconsin Volunteers, and was mustered out as first lieutenant; graduated from the University of Michigan in 1866 and from its law department in 1867; was admitted to the bar in 1868 and commenced practice in Kenosha; district attorney for Kenosha County 1870-1876; mayor of Kenosha 1876; member, State assembly 1879; member, State senate 1880-1882; moved to Racine, Wis., and six years later made Milwaukee his home; elected as a Republican to the United States Senate and served from March 4, 1899, to March 3, 1905; was not a candidate for reelection in 1905; chairman, Committee on Transportation Routes to the Seaboard (Fifty-sixth Congress), Committee on the Census (Fifty-seventh and Fifty-Eighth Congresses); appointed United States district judge for the eastern district of Wisconsin by President Theodore Roosevelt in 1905, and served until his death in Milwaukee, Wis., October 7, 1911; interment in the City Cemetery, Kenosha, Wis.

R

RAE, CHARLOTTE, (1926-), ne Lubotsky, is a stage, film and television actress.

Born in Milwaukee, Wisconsin on April 22, 1926, Rae received a B.S. degree from Northwestern University.

Rae began her career on the stage, making her Broadway debut in the play *Three Wishes for Jamie.* She continued to do a succession of plays that included: *The Time of the Cuckoo, The Threepenny Opera, The Golden Apple, The Littlest Revue, L'il Abner, The Beggars Opera, Pickwick Papers, Henry IV, Romeo and Juliet, Come Back Little Sheba* and *Boom Boom Room.*

Some of her film work includes *Hello Down There, Jenny, Hot Rock, Bananas, Rabbit Test,* and *Hair.* However, she is known to most viewers by her television appearances in: *Car 54, Where Are You?, Sesame Street, The Rich Little Show, Hot L Baltimore, Queen of the Stardust Ballroom,* and her two popular series'--*Diff'rent Strokes* and *The Fact of Life,* with the latter running for six years.

Rae was married and divorced from John Strauss. She has two sons.

RANDALL, ALEXANDER (1819-1872), postmaster-general and sixth governor of Wisconsin, was born in Ames, New York, October 31, 1819, the son of Phineas Randall. Alexander attended college, studied law, and began the practice of his profession in 1840, in Waukesha. He was appointed postmaster at Waukesha, and in 1847 was elected a member of the convention that framed the Constitution. In 1855 Randall was a member of the State Assembly, an unsuccessful competitor for the Attorney-Generalship, and was chosen judge, to fill an unexpired term of the Milwaukee Circuit Court. In 1857 he was elected Governor of Wisconsin. Re-elected in 1859, he occupied the gubernatorial chair at the outbreak of the war. Randall declared at once the loyalty of Wisconsin to the Union, and the intention of the people to fight for its integrity in such a way as to draw national attention. His prompt and efficient measures augmented the useful service of the state. Randall assembled the Legislature in extra session, but before it could act, he organized the 2nd regiment, using public funds before a lawful appropriation had been made; but when the Legislature convened it upheld him in what he had done. When his term as governor expired in 1861 he contemplated entering the Army, but was prevailed upon by President Lincoln to accept the post of Minister to Italy, where he remained for a year. When he returned home he became first assistant to Postmaster-General Dennison. In 1866 President Johnson appointed Randall Postmaster-General, and he served in that capacity to the end of that administration. Randall died July 25, 1872, in Elmira, New York.

RANKIN, JOSEPH, (1833-1886) a U. S. Representative from Wisconsin; born in Passaic, N.J., September 25, 1833; pursued an academic course; moved to Mishicott, Manitowoc County, Wis., in 1854 and engaged in mercantile pursuits; member of the county board in 1869; member of the State assembly in 1860; during the Civil War enlisted in the Union Army in 1862 and was chosen captain of Company D, Seventy-sixth Regiment, Wisconsin Volunteer Infantry; after the war settled in Manitowoc, Wis.; city clerk of Manitowoc 1866-1871; again a member of the State assembly 1871-1874; served in the State senate 1877-1882; elected as a Democrat to the Forty-eighth and Forty-ninth Congresses and served from March 4, 1883, until his death in Washington, D.C., January 24, 1886; interment in Evergreen Cemetery, Manitowoc, Wis.

RASKIN, ELLEN (1928-1984) was a commercial illustrator and designer whose specialty was children's books.

Born in Milwaukee, Wisconsin on March 13, 1928, she attended the University of Wisconsin from 1945 to 1949.

During her career, Raskin designed more than one thousand book jackets, as well as creating illustrations for numerous magazines and advertisements.

Books that she both wrote and illustrated include: *Nothing Ever Happens on My Block*, 1966; *Songs of Innocence*, two volumes, 1966; *Silly Songs and Sad*, 1967; *Spectacles*, 1968; *Ghost in a Four-Room Apartment*, 1969; *And It Rained*, 1969; *A & The*, 1970; *The World's Greatest Freak Show*, 1971; *Who, Said Sue, Said Whoo?*, 1973; and *He Smokes Too Much*, 1973.

She was the illustrator on: Dylan Thomas, *A Child's Christmas in Wales*, 1959; Molly Cone, *The Jewish*

Sabbath, 1966; Susan Bartlett, *Books*, 1968; and B.K. Weiss, *A Paper Zoo*, 1968; among others.

Raskin also wrote three novels: *The Mysterious Disappearance of Leon (I Mean Noel)*, 1971; *Figgs & Phantoms*, 1974; and *The Tattooed Potato and Other Clues*, 1975.

She was given several awards for her work including the *New York Herald Tribune* Children's Book Week Award (best picture book), 1966, for *Nothing Ever Happens on My Block* and the Newbery Honor Book in 1975 for *Figgs & Phantoms*. In addition, her book *Songs of Innocence* was included in the American Institute of Graphic Arts exhibit of 50 best books of the year in 1966.

She was married twice, the second time to Dennis Flanagan, the editor of *Scientific American*. She had one daughter from her first marriage.

Ellen Raskin died of complications from connective-tissue disease on August 8, 1984.

RAY, NICHOLAS (1911-1979), born Raymond Nicholas Kienzle, was a film director.

Born in Galesville, Wisconsin on August 7, 1911, Ray attended the University of Chicago where he studied architecture under Frank Lloyd Wright. He was also a director for Wright's Taliesin Playhouse from 1935 to 1937.

He continued his theatre directing, meeting and working with such esteemed directors as John Houseman, Elia Kazan and Martin Ritt. Kazan chose Ray to assist him during the filming of *A Tree Grows in Brooklyn* (1945). Ray also worked with Houseman on the early television dramas produced when TV was still a new medium, and continued working with Houseman when the latter was asked to do film production for RKO Studios.

In 1948, Ray began directing, and went on to create several memorable films that included *Knock On Any Door*, 1948; *In a Lonely Place*, 1950; *On Dangerous Ground*, 1950; *Johnny Guitar*, 1954; *Rebel Without a Cause*, 1955; *The True Story of Jesse James*, 1956 (which he only directed part of, walking out on the project before it was finished); *The Savage Innocents*, 1959; *King of Kings*, 1961; *55 Days at Peking*, 1962; *Dreams of Thirteen*, 1976; and *The American Friend*, 1977.

In 1979, he was part of a very personal film documentary entitled *Lightning Over Water*, which dealt with the last few months of his life, during which he was dying of cancer.

Ray was married four times and had four children. He died on June 16, 1979.

REHNQUIST, WILLIAM HUBBS (1924-), is a United States Supreme Court Justice.

Born in Milwaukee, Wisconsin on October 1, 1924, he attended Stanford University, receiving a B.A. degree in 1948. He continued his education at Harvard University, earning an M.A. degree in political science, and was awarded an LL.B. degree from Stanford Law School in 1952 (graduating first in his class).

His first job was as a law clerk for the late Justice Robert H. Jackson, where he worked for eighteen months. Deciding to move to Arizona to practice law, he joined the firm of Evans, Kitchel and Jenckes, then three years later, opened his own office with another lawyer, Keith W. Ragan.

During that time, he started to become involved in politics, drifting toward the ultraconservative faction of the Republican Party. A lawyer acquaintance from those days remembers his impression of Rehnquist: "Unlike a lot of Arizona politicians who tried to follow the public thought, Rehnquist really is a deep philosophical conservative. He apparently just sat down and thought it out and decided intellectually that he is against anything liberal."

In 1957, Rehnquist and Ragan dissolved their partnership, and the following year, he was named as special Arizona state prosecutor, during which time he was involved in bringing state officials to trial for fraud. After working for another law firm, he became partners with former IRS lawyer, James Powers, and continued to become more involved in Arizona politics, meeting such staunch conservatives as Barry Goldwater and Richard Kleindienst. When the latter was named by President Nixon as Deputy Attorney General, Rehnquist was chosen as assistant attorney general and was made head of the Office of Legal Counsel.

During his tenure under Nixon's administration, Rehnquist vigorously defended the President's policies on such controversial issues as wiretapping, pretrial detention, "no-knock" entries, and the Vietnam War, as well as supporting mass arrests of peaceful demonstrators.

In October of 1971, President Nixon named Lewis F. Powell and William Rehnquist as nominees for the position of Associate Justice of the Supreme Court. Powell was readily accepted by most of the Senate, but Rehnquist had a harder time getting approval due to what they felt was his apparent lack of respect for the Bill of Rights, especially regarding the rights of citizens and the civil rights movement. Finally in December of 1971, the Senate voted sixty-eight to twenty-six in favor of the appointment and a month later, both Rehnquist and Powell were sworn in as Associate Justices. Rehnquist remained an Associate Justice until 1986 when he was voted in as Chief Justice.

Rehnquist has contributed numerous articles to national magazines and law journals. From 1943 to 1946, he served in the United States Army Air Force.

Rehnquist has been married to Natalie Cornell since 1953 and the couple have three children.

REID, HELEN ROGERS (1882-1970) was a newspaper publisher.

Born in Appleton, Wisconsin on November 23, 1882, she received an A.B. degree from Barnard College in 1903.

After marrying Ogden Reid who had inherited the New York *Herald Tribune*, she began working as advertising manager for the paper. When her husband died in 1947, Mrs. Reid became president of the newspaper, and chairman of the board, six years later.

Reid was involved in the Women's Suffrage Movement and made sure there were articles and editorials included in her newspaper concerning women's issues.

Helen and Ogden Reid had two children. She died on July 27, 1970.

RENNEBOHM, OSCAR (1889-1968), thirty-first governor of Wisconsin, was born in Leeds, Wisconsin on May 25, 1889, the son of William and Julia (Brandt) Rennebohm. His family moved to Milwaukee, and he attended high school there, graduating in 1908. He worked in a drug store for a year, then entered the University of Wisconsin, Madison, where he studied pharmacy. Upon graduation, in 1911, he worked for a druggist, and then bought a pharmacy. During World War I he attended officer candidate school and was commissioned Ensign. In 1920, he married Mary Fowler. They had one daughter.

Rennebohm entered politics in 1944 when he was elected Lieutenant Governor under Governor Goodland. Both he and Goodland were reelected in 1946, and when the Governor died the following year, Rennebohm became Acting Governor. In 1948, he was officially elected to the office of governor. During his administration Rennebohm supported changes to public education, began a veterans' housing program, and charged the State Building Commission with a new program for construction in the state.

At the end of his term, in 1950, he returned to his pharmaceutical activities. He was president of the Wisconsin Pharmaceutical Association, vice-president of the American Pharmaceutical Association, and treasurer of the National Association of Retail Druggists. He also served on the Board of Regents for the University of Wisconsin. Rennebohm died in Maple Bluff, Wisconsin on October 15, 1968.

REYNOLDS, JOHN W. (1921-), thirty-fifth governor of Wisconsin, was born in Green Bay, Wisconsin on April 4, 1921, the son of John and Madge (Flatley) Reynolds. He attended the University of Wisconsin and graduated in 1942. During World War II, he served in the army infantry where he rose to the rank of master sergeant. He was commissioned in 1944 and sent to the Counter Intelligence Corps where he served until 1946. He was discharged with the rank of first lieutenant. In 1947, he married Patricia Ann Brody. They had three children.

On his discharge from the army, Reynolds studied law at the University of Wisconsin Law School. He graduated in 1949 and began a law practice in Green Bay. In 1950, he ran for the House of Representatives, but was defeated. From 1951-52, he served as district director of the Office of Price Stablization. He was chairman of the Brown County Democratic Party from 1952 to 1956, and from 1955 to 1958, he was the U.S. Commissioner for the Eastern Judicial District of Wisconsin. He also served on the State Administration Commission. Reynolds was elected State Attorney General in 1958. Four years later, he became Governor of Wisconsin. As governor, Reynolds championed civil rights and supported social services. He sought to expand Wisconsin's health, education and welfare programs. He also worked to extend the research facilities of the University of Wisconsin and to attract more businesses to the state.

Reynolds acted as a stand-in for Lyndon Johnson in the 1964 Wisconsin Democratic presidential primary. He emphasized the civil rights issue in his campaign, and won easily over Alabama Governor George Wallace. The same year, Reynolds also sought reelection as governor, but lost to Warren P. Knowles. Reynolds became the U.S. District Judge for Wisconsin's Eastern District in 1965. He remained in that post for many years. In 1967, his wife, Patricia, died. He remarried to Jane Conway. They have two children.

ROTH, TOBIAS ANTON (TOBY), (1938- a U. S. Representative from Wisconsin; born in Strasburg, Emmons County, N.Dak., October 10, 1938; graduated from St.

Mary's High School, Menasha, Wis., 1957; B.A., Marquette University, Milwaukee, 1961; served in the United States Army Reserve, 1962-1969 with rank of lieutenant; realtor; served in the Wisconsin State legislature, 1972-1978; elected as a Republican to the Ninety-sixth and to the four succeeding Congresses (January 3, 1979-January 3, 1989); is a resident of Appleton, Wis.

ROTH, WILLIAM VICTOR, JR., (1921-) a U. S. Representative and a U. S. Senator from Delaware; born in Great Falls, Cascade County, Mont., July 22, 1921; attended the public schools of Helena, Mont.; graduated, University of Oregon 1944; graduated, Harvard Business School 1943; graduated, Harvard Law School 1949; admitted to the California bar in 1950 and the Delaware bar in 1958; served in the United States Army 1943-1946; elected as a Republican to the Ninetieth and Ninety-first Congresses and served from January 3, 1967, until his resignation December 31, 1970; was not a candidate for reelection to the House of Representatives, but was elected in 1970 to the United States Senate for the term commencing January 3, 1971; subsequently appointed January 1, 1971, to fill the vacancy caused by the resignation of John J. Williams for the term ending January 3, 1971; reelected in 1976 and again in 1982 for the term ending January 3, 1989; chairman, Committee on Governmental Affairs (Ninety-seventh through Ninety-ninth Congresses).

S

SALOMON, EDWARD (1830-1909), eighth governor of Wisconsin (1862-64), was born in Stroebeck, Prussia, August 11, 1830, second son of Christoph and Dorthea (Klussmann) Salomon. His father served with distinction in the Prussian army and was severely wounded at the battle of Waterloo. After the Napoleonic wars he became an officer in the civil service of Prussia. The son was educated at the local college and at the University of Berlin. Edward Salomon came to this country in October, 1849, and lived for three years in Manitowoc, Wisconsin, where he devoted himself to the study of the English language. During that time he was successively a school teacher, county surveyor and deputy clerk of the circuit court. In December, 1852, Salomon entered the office of Honorable E. G. Ryan, who was Chief Justice of the Supreme Court of Wisconsin, and on January 25, 1855, was admitted to the bar. He at once formed a legal partnership with Mr. Winfield Smith in Milwaukee. The firm soon reached the front rank of the profession. Politically, Salomon was at first a Democrat, but on the formation of the Republican Party he joined it and in 1860 supported Lincoln for president. The following year he was elected Lieutenant-Governor, and because of the death of the governor, Louis P. Harvey, in April, 1862, Salomon became governor of Wisconisn.

Prominent men in the party feared that because of his youth and inexperience, Salomon was unqualified for his new duties and responsibilities. Salomon, however, quickly allayed these apprehensions; his clearness of understanding, decision of character, and industry soon came to be regarded with the highest favor by all. During the spring and summer of 1862 he organized fourteen new regiments of Wisconsin infantry, besides furnishing a large number of new recruits for the regiments already in the field, and in November of that year he carried into effect the so-called state draft, Wisconsin being the only state in which the measure was enforced without bloodshed. On September 22, 1862, he took part in the convention of the governors of eleven of the free-labor states held in

Altoona, Pennsylvania, for the purpose of considering national affairs, and was one of the signatories to the address, written by Governor John A. Andrew, of Massachusetts, in which the president was warmly commended for his famous emancipation proclamation. He was also the orginator of the law, passed by a special session of the legislature in the summer of 1862, giving to the Wisconsin soldiers in the field the right to vote in elections. Governor Salomon took an active interest in the educational affairs of Wisconsin. A member and for several years president of the Board of Regents of the state university, he was largely instrumental in bringing it from its early deplorable condition to a flourishing state and, while governor, urged the embodiment of the agricultural college and its fund with the university. In June, 1862, the latter institution conferred upon him the honorary degree of LL.D.

In 1869 Salomon moved to New York, where he became identified with the German element and obtained the local business of many of the important financial and other institutions established and managed by wealthy citizens of German extraction. He was also counsel for the German consulate-general in New York. During the early years of his residence in New York the Tweed Ring was at the height of its power, and on the formation of the Committee of Seventy for the purpose of dethroning it, Mr. Salomon became a member and was appointed chairman of the committee on legislation. In October, 1882, he was nominated for the bench of the New York Superior Court by the Citizen's Committee of Fifty and was endorsed by the Republicans and the New York Bar Association, McGovern died on May 16, 1946. He was not married.

SAUERHERING, EDWARD, (1864-1924) a U. S. Representative from Wisconsin; born in Mayville, Dodge County, Wis., June 24, 1864; attended the public schools; was graduated from the Chicago College of Pharmacy in 1885; engaged in the drug business in Chicago, Ill., for three years; returned to Mayville, Wis., and continued in the same business; elected as a Republican to the Fifty-fourth and Fifty-fifth Congresses (March 4, 1895 March 3, 1899); was not a candidate for renomination in 1898 to the Fifty-sixth Congress; superintendent of the commission of public works of Ma.wille 1909-1918; engaged in the construction of waterworks; justice of the peace 1912-1920; died in Mayville, Wis., on March 1, 1924; interment in Graceland Cemetery.

SAWYER, PHILETUS, (1816-1900), senator and lumberman, was born at Whiting, Vermont, September 22, 1816. When he was a year old the family moved to Crown Point, New York, on the west shore of Lake Champlain. His father, a blacksmith, had been impoverished by signing notes for others, and hoped to repair his fortunes in a new locale. The son did his share of the tasks around the home farm and shop and, during the summer he was fourteen, found work at $6 per month. At seventeen he borrowed $100 from an older brother, "bought his time" (until he would be twenty-one) from his father and began to work as a saw-mill hand. Before four years were up he had paid his brother and had given himself two more winter terms in the district school.

Sawyer then operated the mill under contract so successfully that fourteen years after he had purchased his time from his father (1847), he was ready with wife and two sons to emigrate to the great West and take with him $2,200 in cash. An interesting story is connected with the last dollar of this sum. When he was starting on the journey westward, an older brother who lived and died a farmer on the Ticonderoga flats asked Philetus how much he had. Philetus answered that he had $2,000 secured in his belt, but the amount in his pocket he did not know. When he counted it, he found it to be $199. His brother handed him a dollar with the remark "Now remember that when you went to the West you had just 2,200."

Years afterward, when this brother was an old man and was visited at his home by the younger man—then a senator of the United States and possessor of an ample fortune—the latter, thinking he saw some signs of depression or uneasiness in his brother, asked him if he was in debt. The brother confessed he was to the extent of about $1,200 from falling profits at the farm and because of his advancing years. The senator quietly bought up all the claims of the creditors and delivered them to his brother with the remark, "I am not giving you this I am paying my debt to you." "What debt?" he inquired. "Do you remember," said Mr. Sawyer, "giving me a dollar when I started for the West? This is that dollar with the accumulations. I have made about that amount with it."

Sawyer returned to Wisconsin, and settled on a farm in Fond du Lac County, but after two years of short crops sold it and went to the pineries of the Wolf River. At Algoma, now the city of Oshkosh, Wisconsin, he began lumbering, operating a saw-mill on contract (until 1850). Then he rented the mill and operated it on his own account with reasonable success until 1853, when he formed a

116

partnership and purchased the mill. In 1862 Sawyer purchased the interest of his remaining partner at an advance of over $70,000 above his original capital in the business. Sawyer then (1863) took his son, F. P. Sawyer, into the business, and the firm was renamed P. Sawyer & Son. Their mill at Menomonie turned out 150,000 feet of sawed lumber daily.

In 1868 Sawyer explored the head waters of the Wolf River, then bought up large tracts of the best timber land at prices which a few years later would have been merely nominal. By the formation and work of the Keshena Improvement Co., he brought into market millions of feet of the best timber in the state. As the earnings of the enterprise increased, improvements were made and handsome dividends were paid.

In 1849 and subsequently, Sawyer was repeatedly chosen alderman on the City Council of Oshkosh, and in 1857 he was induced to serve in the State Legislature as a Republican respresentative. He declined any further offices, however, until 1861 when he was again chosen to the Legislature. In 1862 he was asked to be the Repulbican candidate for Congress from his congressional district, but declined. From 1863 to 1864 he was mayor of Oshkosh, and in the latter year he was elected as a Republican to the thirty-ninth Congress by about 3,000 majority in a district ordinarily doubtful.

Sawyer took his seat on the first Monday of December, 1865. Congress was at that time confronted with the problems of the reconstruction of the Federal union, of national finance, currency, and the changes in industry brought about by the end of the Civil War. There was work enough to be done not only by statesmen, but by men of clear-headed business qualifications, and financial skill and sagacity. As to Sawyer's success in dealing with these problems, James G. Blaine said of him, in his *Twenty Years in Congress* : "It is easy to supply superlatives in eulogy of popular favorites; but in modest phrases Mr. Sawyer deserves to be ranked among the best men—honest, industrious, generous, true to every tie and to every obligation of life. He remained ten years in the House with constantly increasing influence, and was afterwards promoted to the Senate."

After retiring from Congress March 4, 1875, Sawyer found his private business still prospering under the management of his son. He was a member of the executive committee of the Chicago, St. Paul, Minniapolis & Omaha Railroad Company until 1880, when he servered his connection with it and prepared to visit Europe with his family.

This plan was abandoned, however, and when the Wisconsin Legislature of 1881 met, and the Republican members assembled in caucus to agree upon a candidate, Sawyer was found to be the choice of a large majority. In January Sawyer was elected senator for six years from March 4, 1881. In January, 1887, he was re-elected without opposition in his own party for the term ending 1893. His career in the Senate was marked by the same useful and conscientious discharge of his duties which characterized his term in the House of Representatives.

Senator Sawyer was married, near Crown Point, New York, in 1841, to M. M. Hadley, who died May 21, 1888. Sawyer survived until 1900.

SCHADEBERG, HENRY CART, (1913-1985) a U. S. Representative from Wisconsin; born in Manitowoc, Manitowoc County, Wis., October 12, 1913; graduated from Manitowoc public schools; Carroll College, Waukesha, Wis., B.A., 1938, and Garrett Biblical Institute, Evanston, Ill., B.D., 1941; clergyman; served in the United States Navy as a chaplain from 1943 to 1946 and in the Korean conflict from 1952 to 1953; captain in the United States Naval Reserve until retirement in 1969; elected as a Republican to the Eighty-seventh and Eighty-eighth Congresses (January 3, 1961-January 3, 1965); unsuccessful candidate for reelection in 1964; delegate, Republican State conventions since 1960; delegate, Republican National Convention, 1964; elected to the Ninetieth and Ninety-first Congresses (January 3, 1967-January 3, 1971); unsucessful candidate for reelection in 1970 to the Ninety-second Congress; was a resident of Rockbridge Baths, Va., until his death there December 11, 1985; ashes buried at Hill-Valley Ranch.

SCHAFER, JOHN CHARLES, (1893-1962) a U. S. Representative from Wisconsin; born in Milwaukee, Wis., May 7, 1893; attended the public schools of Wauwatosa and West Allis High School; employed in the office of the Allis-Chalmers Co.; during the First World War enlisted in the Thirteenth Engineers on May 24, 1917, and served twenty-two months in France; engaged as a locomotive engineer on the Chicago & North Western Railroad; member of Wauwatosa School Board, district No. 11; member of the State assembly in 1921; elected as a

118

Republican to the Sixtyeighth and to the four succeeding Congresses (March 4, 1923-March 3, 1933); unsuccessful candidate for reelection in 1932 and for election in 1934 to the Seventy-fourth Congress and in 1936 to the Seventy-fifth Congress; elected to the Seventy-sixth Congress (January 3, 1939-January 3, 1941); unsuccessful candidate for reelection in 1940 to the Seventy-seventh Congress and for election in 1942 to the Seventy-eighth Congress; unsuccessfully contested the election of Thaddeus F.B. Wasielewski in the Seventy-eighth Congress; unsuccessful candidate for election in 1952 to the Eighty-third Congress, in 1954 to the Eighty-fourth Congress, and in 1957 for the senatorial nomination to fill a vacancy; engaged in the sale of automotive electrical equipment and in the insurance business in Oak Park, Ill.; died in Pewaukee, Wis., June 9, 1962; interment in Arlington Park, Milwaukee, Wis.

SCHICKEL, RICHARD WARREN (1933-) is a writer and film critic.

Born in Milwaukee, Wisconsin on February 10, 1933, he received a B.S. degree from the University of Wisconsin in 1955.

He first began his career as a reporter for *Sports Illustrated* in 1956. A year later he became senior editor at *Look* magazine. In 1960 he worked in the same capacity for *Show*, becoming the magazine's book columnist in 1963. Later that year, Schickel quit his job in order to freelance, then in 1965 he became *Life* magazine's film critic where he stayed until 1972. A year later he became the film critic for *Time* magazine.

Schickel is the author of several books, including: *The World of Carnegie Hall*, 1960; *The Stars*, 1962; *The History of an Art and an Institution*, 1964; *The Gentle Knight*, 1964; *The Disney Version*, 1968; *The World of Goya*, 1968; *Second Sight: Notes on Some Movies*, 1972; *His Picture in the Papers*, 1974; *Harold Lloyd: The Shape of Laughter*, 1974; *The Men Who Made the Movies*, 1975; *Cary Grant, A Celebration*, 1984; *D.W. Griffith: an American Life*, 1984; and *Intimate Strangers: The Culture of Celebrity*, 1985; among others.

He has also been involved as writer, director and/or producer of several television specials such as: *The Men Who Made the Movies*, 1973; *Life Goes to the Movies*, 1976; *Funny Business*, 1978; and *James Cagney: That Yankee Doodle Dandy*, 1981; among others.

Schickel is a member of the National Society of Film Critics and the New York Film Critics. He married Julia Whedon in 1961 and the couple have two daughters.

SCHMEDEMAN, ALBERT G. (1864-1946), twenty-eighth governor of Wisconsin, was born on November 25, 1864 in Madison, Wisconsin, the son of Henry and Wilhelmina (Camien) Schmedeman. He attended Northwestern Business College and upon graduation began work for the clothing firm of Olson, Winder and Veerhusen as a bundle boy. He eventually became a member of the firm and it was reorganized as Winder, Grinde and Schmedeman. In 1892, he married Katherine Regan, and they had two children.

In 1904, Schmedeman was elected Alderman for the city of Madison. He served two terms, then became City Fire and Police Commissioner and a member of the Board of Education. He ran for Congress in 1910, but lost the election. He also tried for mayor of Madison in 1912, but was defeated. In 1913, he served as treasurer of the Democratic State Committee and supported Woodrow Wilson. Wilson reciprocated by appointing him Minister to Norway, a position he held for the next eight years. Schmedeman returned to Wisconsin and entered into his interest with the National Guardian Life Insurance Company. In 1925, he was elected Mayor of Madison, and served until 1932, when he won the governorship. He had run a previous unsuccessful campaign for the governor's office in 1928. Now, in 1932, his administration was taken up with the problems of the Great Depression. Schmedeman ordered the banks closed, and attempted to secure a moratorium on farm and home loans. He also sent state troops to maintain order during dairy strikes. During his term the Prohibition Enforcement Act was repealed.

Schmedeman ran for a second term in 1934. That summer, while dedicating Rib Mountain State Park at Wausau, he fell and hurt his foot. Neglecting to care for it properly in the midst of his political campaign, he developed gangrene, and eventually lost the leg. He was defeated in the election by Progressive Philip La Follette; however, the legislature voted him compensation for his injury. In 1935, President Roosevelt named him Federal Housing Administrator for Wisonsin. He retired from this post in 1942, in poor health. Albert Schmedeman died in Madison on November 26, 1946.

SCHNEIDER, GEORGE JOHN, (1877-1939) a U. S. Representative from Wisconsin; born in the town of Grand Chute, Outagamie County; Wis., October 30, 1877; moved to Appleton with his parents, attended the public schools of Appleton, Wis.; learned the trade of paper making; vice president of the International Brotherhood of Paper Makers 1909-1927; member of the executive board of the Wisconsin State Federation of Labor 1921-1928; elected as a Republican to the Sixty-eighth through Seventy-second Congresses (March 4, 1923-March 3, 1933); unsuccessful candidate for reelection in 1932 to the Seventy-third Congress; elected as a Progressive to the Seventy-fourth and Seventy-fifth Congresses (January 3, 1935- January 3, 1939); unsuccessful candidate for reelection in 1938 to the Seventy-sixth Congress; resumed labor activities and died in Toledo, Ohio, March 12, 1939, while attending a labor meeting; interment in Riverside Cemetery, Appleton, Wis.

SCHREIBER, MARTIN J. (1939-), thirty-eighth governor of Wisconsin, was born in Milwaukee on April 8, 1939, the son of Martin and Emeline (Kurz) Schreiber. He received his education at Valparaiso University, the University of Wisconsin, and Marquette University, where he earned an LL.B. degree in 1964. In 1961, he married Elaine Thaney. They had four children.

In 1962, while still at the university, Schreiber was elected to the Wisconsin Senate. He was reelected in 1964 and 1968. Schreiber ran for lieutenant governor in 1966, but lost the election. He served as Democratic Caucus Chair in 1967 and 1969; then, in 1970, he ran once again for lieutenant governor on the Democratic ticket with Patrick Lucey. Schreiber won, becoming the first lieutenant governor in Wisconsin elected to a four year term. In 1974, he was reelected, and in 1977, when Lucey resigned to become Ambassador to Mexico, Schreiber became Acting Governor. In the remainder of the four year governor's term, he sought to continue efforts started by Lucey. He signed into law an income tax relief bill for low income and elderly persons, a new code of ethics for public employees, tighter lobbying regulations, a tough drunk-driver law, and although he originally disapproved it, a bill to prohibit the use of state funds for non-therapeutic abortions. Schreiber ran for governor in 1978, but was defeated by Lee Sherman Dreyfus. He subsequently moved to Stevens Point where he became vice-president of Sentry Insurance. He tried for

121

the governorship once again in the 1982 election, but was defeated in the primary by Anthony Earl. Schreiber then resumed work with Sentry Insurance.

SENSENBRENNER, FRANK JAMES, (1943-) Jr., a U. S. Representative from Wisconsin; born in Chicago, Ill., June 14, 1943; graduated from Milwaukee Country Day School (high school), 1961; A.B.. Stanford University, California, 1965; staff member to United States Representative J. Arthur Younger, California, J.D., University of Wisconsin Law School, Madison, admitted to the Wisconsin bar in 1968 and commenced practice in Cedarburg; private practice of law, 1970-1975; served in the Wisconsin assembly, 1969-1975; State senate, 1975-1979 and was assistant minority leader, 1977-1979; delegate, Wisconsin State Republican conventions, 1965-1988; elected as a Republican to the Ninety-sixth and to the four succeeding Congresses (January 3, 1979-January 3, 1989); is a resident of Menomonee Falls, Wis.

SHAW, GEORGE BATTEN, (1854-1894) a U. S. Representative from Wisconsin; born in Alma, Allegany County, N.Y., on March 12, 1854; moved to Eau Claire, Wis., in 1856 with his father; attended the public schools and was graduated from the International Business College, Chicago, Ill., in 1871; engaged in the lumber manufacturing business; member of the Common Council of Eau Claire 1876-1887; mayor of Eau Claire in 1888 and 1889; delegate to the Republican National Convention in 1884; supreme chancellor of the Knights of Pythias of the World from July 1890 to August 1892; elected as a Republican to the Fifty-third Congress and served from March 4, 1893, until his death in Eau Claire, Wis., August 27, 1894; interment in Lake View Cemetery.

SIMON, HERBERT ALEXANDER (1916-?) is a social scientist.

Born in Milwaukee, Wisconsin on June 15, 1916, he attended the University of Chicago, receiving an A.B. degree in 1936 and a Ph.D. degree in 1943.

In 1938, Simon got a staff job at the International City Managers' Association where he was assistant editor of the book *Public Management and Municipal Year Book*. A year later he became director of administrative measurement studies at the University of California's

Bureau of Public Administration in Berkeley. Between 1942 and 1949, Simon held various positions at the Illinois Institute of Technology, starting as assistant professor and later becoming professor of political science as well as head of the department of political and social science. In 1949, Simon was professor of administration at the Carnegie Institute of Technology, becoming professor of administration and psychology in 1962. Three years later he became professor of computer service and psychology at Richard King Mellon.

Besides being a distinguished lecturer at various universities such as Princeton, Northwestern, Harvard and the Massachusetts Institute of Technology, Simon has been a consultant to several agencies including the Cowles Foundation for Research in Economics and the RAND Corporation. He has also been Chairman of the Division of Behavioral Sciences for the National Research Council and a member of numerous organizations such as: the President's Science Advisory Committee; the American Psychological Association; the American Society for Computing Machinery; the American Sociological Association; and the American Association of University Professors; among others.

A partial list of Simon's numerous writings includes: (with C.E. Ridley) *Measuring Municipal Activities*, 1938; *Fiscal Aspects of Metropolitan Consolidation*, 1943; (with others) *Technique of Municipal Administration*, 1947; *Administrative Behavior*, 1947; *Models of Man*, 1958; *the New Science of Management Decision*, 1960; *The Sciences of the Artificial*, 1969;--and as contributor: *Research Frontiers in Politics and Government*, 1955; *The State of the Social Sciences*, 1956; *Research in Industrial Human Relations*, 1957; *Labor Problems: Cases and Readings*, 1959; *Control of the Mint*, 1961; *Automation: Implications for the Future*, 1962; *Contemporary Approaches to Creative Thinking*, 1962; and *Mind and Cosmos*, 1966; among many others.

Simon is married to educational researcher, Dorothea Pye, and the couple have three children.

SLAYTON, DONALD KENT (1924-), known to his friends as "Deke," is a former astronaut and design engineer.

Born in Sparta, Wisconsin on March 1, 1924, he attended the University of Michigan. By doubling up on his courses, Slayton was able to finish college in two years, receiving a B.Aero. Engineering degree in 1949.

After serving in the United States Army Air Force as a pilot from 1942 to 1946, during which he flew in bombing missions over Europe and Japan, Slayton became a design engineer for the Boeing Aircraft comapny in 1949. In 1951, he rejoined the Air Force as commanding captain, becoming a major in 1959 and resigning in 1963. During his time in the service he was a fighter pilot and maintenance officer in Germany (1952-1955), as well as a fighter test pilot at Edwards Air Force Base in California (1955-1959).

In 1959, he became a member of Project Mercury, the manned space flight program for NASA, and was one of the first seven astronauts named to explore outer space. Unfortunately, Slayton was found to have an irregular heartbeat and he was denied the initial glory experienced by the other astronauts in the beginning stages of the space program.

However, Slayton remained an important part of the program after he was named as the Manned Spacecraft Center's chief of flight crew operations, during which he helped decide who would fly in the subsequent space flights.

Although Slayton enjoyed the work immensely ("I guess next to flying them, I've probably had the best job anybody in this outfit could have."), he was determined to be one of those who was doing the flying. He got himself in peak physical condition by giving up liquor, cigarettes and coffee and starting an exercise regimen. His perserverance paid off, as he was reinstated to active status in 1972, and was a member of the Apollo crew that made a rendezvous (and subsequent docking) with the Russian Soyuz spacecraft in 1975.

From 1975 until 1977, Slayton was manager of the Space Shuttle Approach and Landing Test, then worked in the same capacity for the Space Shuttle Orbital Flight Test from 1978 to 1982. He became president of Space Service Inc. in 1982.

Slayton has been married twice, to Marjorie Lunney, and currently to Bobbie Osborn. He has one son.

SMITH, GERALD LYMAN KENNETH (1898-1976) was a clergyman whose fiery speeches and extreme right-wing political views kept him in the public eye for most of his adult life.

Born in Pardeeville, Wisconsin on February 27, 1898, sources vary as to his schooling. One source says he graduated from Valparaiso University, Indianapolis; another says it was Indianapolis' Butler College.

Smith came from a long line of "hellfire and brimstone" preachers. Once again, sources differ as to how he began his career as a preacher; however, it is known that in 1928 he became head of King's Highway Church in Schreveport, Louisiana.

Smith ended his association with the church after he met Huey "Kingfish" Long, whom Smith greatly admired. After Long won the governorship of the State of Louisiana, Smith went to work for him full-time and created what he called the "Share-Our-Wealth Society." With his persuasive speaking style, he convinced thousands of people that Huey Long would attach levies on the large bank accounts of the wealthy and later divide and spread the wealth to the less well-off. People who "joined" the club were not asked for any dues; instead they received a badge just by signing and sending in a card. It was also suggested to them that they form their own little groups and elect a president and secretary. Smith, who got paid $650 a week for his efforts, almost singlehandedly got Long the kind of support and recognition he wanted.

Smith's power was diminished considerably after the assassination of Huey Long in September of 1935. He demanded an official investigation into the politician's death and publicly blamed some members of the Roosevelt administration for the murder. On the other hand, he had a strong conviction that he could take Long's place, saying: "Six million people have written me to say, 'You lead. I'll follow you.' And when the time is ripe, when chaos comes, I'll lead them, all right." But members of Long's camp would not support him in any way and soon after Long's death, they made their peace with President Roosevelt.

Smith would not go away quietly, however, and made his opinions known at a "rebel rally" held by Georgia's Governor Talmadge. With great defiance, Smith pronounced: "We're going to drive that cripple out of the White House--and we're going to do it in 1936." "Roosevelt is rapidly becoming the most despised President in the history of the country," he continued. "He gave us the Russian primer and cursed the Bible...He and his gang are in the death rattle. We have only to put the cloth of the ballot over his dead mouth!"

Through the years, Smith continued his "rabble-rousing" ways, passionately supporting capitalism ("Public ownership? Not in anything!") and isolationism, speaking at meetings of the Keep America Out of War Committee. He was also vehemently against Communism, forming the Committee of One Million to provide a "nationalist front" against it.

SMITH, LAWRENCE HENRY

Smith continued to spread his own personal propaganda on various political subjects by publishing the pamphlet *The Hoop of Steel,* and a magazine entitled *The Cross and The Flag.* In April of 1942, he decided to run for the Republican Senate seat for the State of Michigan, preaching that "old-fashioned, Christian, American people" would be the ones to vote him into office. Smith did not receive his hoped for nomination; however he garnered votes from nearly 100,000 Michigan supporters. Inspired by this show of confidence, Smith created the America First Party, which eventually faded out.

In a 1936 speech, he summed up his basic philosophy: "They tell me that I mustn't refer to our sacred flag. That would be rabble-rousing. They tell me that I must not speak of our glorious Constitution. That would be rabble-rousing. They say to me that I mustn't quote from the Holy Book, our Christian Bible. But let me tell you, friends, that if it is rabble-rousing to praise the flag and the Constitution, and to love the Bible, then I can only pray to God that in His infinite wisdom He will make me the greatest rabble-rouser in the United States."

Smith was married to Eleanor Sorenson. He died on April 15, 1976.

SMITH, LAWRENCE HENRY, (1892-1958) a U. S. Representative from Wisconsin; born in Racine, Boone County, Wis., September 15, 1892; attended the public schools and the State Teachers College, Milwaukee, Wis.; graduated from the Marquette University Law School, Milwaukee, Wis., in 1923; was admitted to the bar the same year and commenced the practice of law in Racine, Wis.; during the First World War served as a first lieutenant of Infantry, Thirty-second Division, 1917-1919; elected as a Republican to the Seventy-seventh Congress to fill the vacancy caused by the death of Stephen Bolles; reelected to the Seventy-eighth and to the seven succeeding Congresses and served from August 29, 1941, until his death in the United States Capitol, Washington, D.C., January 22, 1958; interment in West Lawn Memorial Park, Racine, Wis.

SMITH, RED (1905-1982), born Walter Wellesley Smith, was once described as "the best sports reporter in the business."

Born in Green Bay, Wisconsin on September 25, 1905, (or as he once joked, "about eleven million words ago"), graduated from the University of Notre Dame in 1927.

Smith began his newspaper career soon after, becoming a general news writer for the Milwaukee *Sentinel*. A year later, he moved to St. Louis and became a copyreader for the former *Star* newspaper (what is now the *Star-Times*). Smith eventually worked his way up to sportswriter. After writing for the *Star* for several years, he moved to Philadelphia in 1936 and wrote a sports column for the *Record*, this time with his own byline.

A few years later, he was asked to join the New York *Herald Tribune* by the paper's sports editor, Stanley Woodward, who called Smith "the best newspaper writer in the country." His *Views of Sport* was printed six days a week and according to Smith, the columns came out "in little drops of blood."

Always bluntly honest about his lack of talent in sports as a child, he nevertheless was widely praised for his knowledge of such games as boxing, baseball, football and horse-racing.

His column was the springboard for several other ventures, including articles for such magazines as the *Saturday Evening Post, Sports Illustrated,* and *Colliers* ; and the books *Out of the Red, Views of Sports,* and *The Sporting World of Red Smith.* In addition, Smith was involved in television work, narrating a twenty-six program series concerning little known facts about sports, and appearing on Edward R. Murrow's *Person to Person.*

Later in his career, Smith began working for the New York *Times*, writing the column "Sports of the Times." He won several prestigious awards during his career, including the National Headliners Club Award in 1945, the Grantland Rice Memorial Award in 1956, and the Pulitzer Prize for commentary in 1976.

While describing himself in unflattering terms--"a seedy amateur with watery eyes behind glittering glasses, a retiring chin, a hole in his frowzy haircut, and a good deal of dandruff on his shoulders," his writing style received only the highest praise, with *Time* magazine calling Smith "the most influential and admired sportswriter of our time."

Smith was married twice, to Catherine Cady and Phyllis Weiss, and had two children from his first marriage.

Red Smith died on January 15, 1982.

SOMERS, PETER J., (1850-1924) a U. S. Representative from Wisconsin; born at Menominee Falls, Waukesha County, Wis., April 12, 1850; attended the common schools, the Whitewater Normal School, and the Waukesha

Academy; studied law; was admitted to the bar in 1874 and commenced practice in Milwaukee, Wis.; attorney of the city of Milwaukee 1882-1884; elected to the common council in 1890, and upon its organization became its president; mayor of Milwaukee 1890- 1893; elected as a Democrat to the Fifty-third Congress to fill the vacancy caused by the resignation of John L. Mitchell and served from August 27, 1893, to March 3, 1895; was not a candidate for renomination in 1894; resumed the practice of law in Milwaukee; moved to Reno, Nev., in 1905 and continued the practice of law; chairman of the State Democratic central committee from 1907 to 1909; appointed district judge of Esmeralda County in 1908, and elected in 1910 for the term ending January 1, 1914; again engaged in the practice of law; died in Los Angeles, Calif., February 15, 1924; interment in Calvary Cemetery.

STEWART, ALEXANDER, (1829-1912) a U. S. Representative from Wisconsin; born in Fredericton, York County, New Brunswick, Canada, September 12, 1829; attended the common schools of his native city; moved to Marathon County, Wis., in 1849, and settled where the city of Wausau is now located; engaged in the lumber business; delegate to the Republican National Convention in 1884; elected as a Republican to the Fiftyfourth, Fifty-fifth, and Fifty-sixth Congresses (March 4, 1895-March 3, 1901); was not a candidate for renomination in 1900 to the Fifty-seventh Congress; resided in Washington, D.C., until his death on May 24, 1912; interment in Pine Grove Cemetery, Wausau, Wis.

SUMNER, DANIEL HADLEY, (1837-1903) a U. S. Representative from Wisconsin; born in Malone, Franklin County, N.Y., September 15, 1837; moved to Michigan in 1843 with his parents, who settled in Richland; attended the common schools and Prairie Seminary, Richland, Mich.; studied law; was admitted to the bar in 1868 and commenced practice in Kalamazoo, Mich.; moved to Oconomowoc, Wis., in 1868 and practiced law; also published the La Belle Mirror; moved to Waukesha, Wis., in 1870 and continued the practice of his profession; town superintendent of schools; member of the county board of supervisors; district attorney of Waukesha County in 1876 and 1877; elected as a Democrat to the Forty eighth Congress (March 4, 1883-March 3, 1885); was not a candidate for renomination in 1884; resumed the practice of law; died in Waukesha, Wis., May 29, 1903; interment in Prairie Home Cemetery.

T

THILL, LEWIS DOMINIC, (1903- 1975) a U. S. Representative from Wisconsin; born in Milwaukee, Wis., October 18, 1903; attended the public and parochial schools and was graduated from Marquette University, Milwaukee, Wis., in 1926; attended Harvard Graduate School, and Northwestern University, Evanston, Ill.; was graduated from the law department of the University of Wisconsin at Madison in 1931; was admitted to the bar in 1932 and commenced practice in Milwaukee, Wis.; elected as a Republican to the Seventy-sixth and the Seventy-seventh Congresses (January 3, 1939-January 3, 1943); unsuccessful candidate for reelection in 1942 to the Seventy-eighth Congress and for election in 1944 to the Sevent-ninth Congress; engaged in real estate and investment business; resided in San Diego, Calif., where he died May 6, 1975; entombment in Holy Cross Mausoleum.

THOMAS, ORMSBY BRUNSON, (1832-1904) a U. S. Representative from Wisconsin; born in Sandgate, Bennington County, Vt., August 21, 1832; moved with his parents to Wisconsin in 1836; attended the common schools and Burr Seminary, Manchester, Vt.; was graduated from the National Law School, Poughkeepsie, keepsie, N.Y., in 1856; was admitted to the bar in Albany, N.Y., in 1856 and commenced practice in Prairie do Chien, Wis.; district attorney of Crawford County, Wis.; served in the Union Army during the Civil War as captain of Company D, Thirty-first Regiment, Wisconsin Volunteer Infantry; member of the State assembly in 1862, 1865, and 1867; served in the State senate in 1880 and 1881; elected as a Republican to the Forty-ninth, Fiftieth, and Fifty-first Congresses (March 4, 1885-March 3, 1891); chairman, Committee on War Claims (Fifty-first Congress); was an unsuccessful candidate for reelection in 1890 to the Fifty-second Congress; resumed the practice of law in Prairie do Chien, Wis., and died there October 24, 1904; interment in Evergreen Cemetery.

THOMPSON, TOMMY G. (1941-), forty-first governor of Wisconsin, was born November 19, 1941 in Elroy, Wisconsin. He attended elementary school and high school in his home town, then moved to Madison where he enrolled in the University of Wisconsin. In 1963 Thompson completed his undergraduate degree in political science and history. He then entered law school and graduated with a J.D. degree in 1966. He also served as a captain in the U.S. Army Reserves.

After graduation, Thompson began to work as an attorney and became involed in politics. He was elected to the State Assembly in 1966, and during the 1973 session was named Assistant Minority leader. In December, 1981 he became the Republican Floor Leader, a position he held until his election as Wisconsin's 41st governor in November, 1986.

Thompson has been a member of numerous organizations, including the State Bar Association, Juneau County Bar Association, and the Juneau County Republican Party. He and his wife, Sue Ann, have three children.

THOMSON, VERNON WALLACE, (1905- a U. S. Representative from Wisconsin; born in Richland Center, Richland County, Wis., November 5, 1905; graduated from Richland Center High School in 1923; attended Carroll College in Waukesha, 1923- 1925; graduated from University of Wisconsin in 1927; taught at Viroqua High School, 1927-1929; graduated from the University of Wisconsin Law School in 1932; engaged in private practice of law, Richland Center, Wis., 1932-1951; assistant district attorney of Richland County, 1933-1935, and city attorney, 1933-1937, and again, 1942-1944; mayor of Richland Center from April 1944 to February 1951; member of the State assembly, 1935-1951, serving as speaker, 1939- 1945, and as Republican floor leader, 1945-1951; State attorney general, 1951-1957; Governor of Wisconsin from January 7, 1957, to January 5, 1959; delegate, Republican National Conventions, 1936, 1940, 1952, and 1956; elected as a Republican to the Eighty-seventh Congress; reelected to the six succeeding Congresses and served from January 3, 1961, until his resignation December 31, 1974; unsuccessful candidate for reelection in 1974 to the Ninety-fourth Congress; member, Federal Election Commission, April 1975 to June 1979 and January 1981 to December 1981; was a resident of

McLean, Va., until his death in Washington, D.C., on April 2, 1988; interment in Richland Center Cemetery, Richland Center, Wis.

TOLAND, JOHN WILLARD (1912-?) is an author and historian.

Born in La Crosse, Wisconsin on June 29, 1912, he graduated from Williams College, receiving a B.A. degree in 1936. He also studied for a year at Yale Drama School.

His first book, *Ships in the Sky* was published in 1957. He authored numerous other non-fiction works, including: *Battle: the Story of the Bulge*, 1959; *But Not in Shame*, 1961; *The Dillinger Days*, 1963; *The Flying Tigers*, 1963; *The Last 100 Days*, 1966; *The Battle of the Bulge*, 1966; *The Rising Sun*, 1970; *Adolf Hitler*, 1976; *Hitler, The Pictorial Documentary of His Life*, 1978; *No Man's Land*, 1980; and *Infamy*, 1982.

In addition, he wrote two novels, *Gods of War*, 1985, and *Occupation*, 1987, and has been a contributor to several major magazines, including *Reader's Digest*, *Life*, *Look*, *Saturday Evening Post* and *American Heritage*, among others.

He has been given several awards through the years, such as the Van Wyck Brooks award, the Overseas Press Club's Foreign Affairs awards (three-time winner), and the Pulitzer Prize for non-fiction for *Adolph Hitler*.

Toland has been married twice and has three daughters.

TRACY, SPENCER (1900-1967), motion picture actor, was born in Milwaukee on April 5, 1900, the son of John and Carrie (Brown) Tracy. As a young student he liked to skip class, and he attended some fifteen schools before finishing grade school at St. Rosa's Parochial School. He was friends with Bill O'Brien (later known to movie-goers as Pat O'Brien), who lived on his block. When World War I started, Tracy quit high school and followed Bill O'Brien into the Navy. Though he "wanted to see the world," he was never sent into combat, and remained at the Norfolk Naval Base throughout the war. After his service, he finished high school and entered Ripon College where he completed three semesters. While at Ripon, he became interested in dramatics. Tracy went to New York and to study at the American Academy of Dramatic Art, but soon ran out of funds and had to quit and find work. He pounded the pavement on Broadway and garnered small roles in several plays.

In 1928, in the cast of a play in White Plains, New York, Tracy met leading lady Louise Treadwell, and within weeks they were married. Tracy's first notable role came in 1930 when he starred as Killer Mears in *The Last Mile.* Soon after, he went to Hollywood where he began his long career in film. He starred in such famous films as *The Power and the Glory* (1933); *Stanley and Livingstone* (1939); *Northwest Passage* (1940); *Edison the Man* (1940); *Dr. Jekyll and Mr. Hyde* (1941); *Woman of the Year* (1942); *Tortilla Flat* (1942); *Keeper of the Flame* (1943); *Thirty Seconds Over Tokyo* (1943); *Bad Day at Black Rock* (1955); and *The Old Man and the Sea* (1958). He won Oscars for best actor as the Portuguese fisherman in *Captains Courageous* in 1937, and for his role as Father Flanagan in *Boys' Town* in 1938.

Spencer Tracy starred in Hollywood films for over thirty years. He died June 10, 1967.

TURNER, FREDERICK JACKSON (1861-1932) was an American historian, educator and author.

Born in Portage, Wisconsin on November 14, 1861, he attended the University of Wisconsin, graduating in 1884. He returned to the University, earning his master's degree in 1888, then continued his education for a year at The Johns Hopkins University, receiving his Ph.D. degree in 1890.

The year before, he became a faculty member at the University of Wisconsin, and in 1892, Turner was named professor of American History. He stayed at Wisconsin until 1910, at which time he became professor of history at Harvard University, teaching there until 1924, then becoming professor-emeritus. He spent the years of 1927-28 as a research associate at the Henry E. Huntington Library.

In July of 1893, at a meeting of the American Historical Association, during the World Columbian Exposition in Chicago, Turner delivered a paper to the group entitled *The Significance of the Frontier in American History* which made quite an impression due to its unique view of American development. While other intellectuals had written on the same subject, emphasizing the importance of Anglo-Saxon political institutions, Turner's viewpoint dealt with the theory that American intelligence and ingenuity came from the struggles endured in trying to tame and make a life in the West. In his writings he claimed that American history was "a series of social evolutions recurring in differing geographic basins across a raw continent."

He continued his writing in this vein, publishing *The Rise of the New West, 1819-1829*, 1906, and *The Frontier in American History*, 1920, which was a collection of papers on the subject. His other works include: *The Significance of Sections in American History*, 1932 (which garnered a Pulitzer Prize for American History), *The United States, 1830-1850: The Nation and Its Sections*, (published posthumously in 1935), and *Early Writings*, (published posthumously in 1938).

Turner was married to Caroline Mae Sherwood and the couple had three children. He died on March 14, 1932.

TWINING, NATHAN FARRAGUT (1897-1982) was a United States Air Force officer.

Born in Monroe, Wisconsin on October 11, 1897, Twining attended various military schools. However, immediately after high school, he trained to become a member of the Oregon National Guard. In June of 1917, he matriculated at the United States Military Academy at West Point, graduating in November of the following year.

After being commissioned a second lieutenant, he was sent to Germany during World War I. Upon his return in 1919, he attended the Fort Benning Infantry School, graduating a year later. He continued his schooling in 1923 at the Primary Flying School at Brooks Field in Texas and later at the Kelly Field, Texas Advanced Flying School where he received his pilot's license in 1924. Twining became a flight instructor and was eventually transferred to the Air Service (what would later become the Army Air Corps).

In 1935, Twining attained the rank of captain and enrolled in the Air Force Tactical School at Maxwell Field, Alabama. From there he immediately entered the Command and General Staff School at Fort Leavenworth, Kansas. In the summer of 1937, he became the Air Corps technical supervisor at the San Antonio Air Depot at Duncan Field, Texas.

In August of 1940, he was transferred to Washington, D.C. to work in the office of the Chief of Air Corps, and was given the rank of major. His initial position was that of assistant chief of the Inspection Division, and he was later made chief of the Technical Inspection Section.

At the beginning of World War II, Twining was appointed assistant executive in the Army Air Forces Chief of Staff office, later becoming director of War Organization and Movements at the same location. In August of 1942, he was named chief of staff of both the ground and air Army

Forces in the South Pacific. During one of his combat missions, a B-17 bomber, carrying Twining and fourteen of his men, was forced to make an emergency landing due to a tropical storm. The group spent the next six days on the Coral Sea in life rafts, surviving on the fish they were able to catch. Upon his return to safety, Twining devised a "memorandum of suggested needs for forced landing," that would hopefully be implemented for any future emergencies.

Twining was given the temporary rank of commander, Air craft, Solomon Islands, which gave him responsibility and "tactical control of all Army, Navy, Marine and Allied Air Forces in the South Pacific." After his stint was over, he was praised by Admiral William F. Halsey, Jr. who said: "It was his force which completely wiped out the effective Japanese air strength on Bougainville." His other commands during that time included the 15th Air Force, replacing the reassigned Major General James H. Doolittle, as well as the Mediterranean Strategic Air Forces.

When the war in Europe came to a close, Twining returned to Washington, D.C. and replaced Major General Curtis E. LeMay who was responsible for the 20th Air Force in the Pacific. With this new command, Twining was in charge of the B-29 bombers that ultimately dropped the atom bombs on Nagasaki and Hiroshima.

Upon the surrender of the Japanese government, Twining was assigned to various posts such as the headquarters of the Continental Air Force at Bolling Field in Washington, D.C.; Air Material Command at Wright Field, Ohio; the Alaskan Command; and Air Force Headquarters in Washington.

He was given the appointment of Vice-Chief of Staff in 1950, and two years later, when Air Chief of Staff, Lieutenant General Hoyt S. Vandenberg was hospitalized, Twining was called in to take his place. According to one source, he "ran the Air Force in all but name, distinguished himself for even-handedness and loyalty to Vandenberg's policies." When Vandenberg gave notice of his resignation from the post in May of 1953, Twining was named as Air Chief of Staff by President Dwight D. Eisenhower. From 1957 to 1960, Twining served as Chairman of the Joint Chiefs of Staff.

Nathan Twining was married to Maude McKeever and the couple had three children. He died at Lakeland Air Force Base in Texas on March 29, 1982.

U

U'REN, WILLIAM SIMON (1859-1949) was a lawyer and political reformer.

Born in Lancaster, Wisconsin on January 10, 1859, his family moved to Nebraska, then Colorado where U'ren studied law in college. He passed the Colorado Bar in 1881 and worked as a lawyer for the next five years.

Suffering from ill health, he gave up law for a time and traveled to various places, working at different jobs such as being a foreman on a Hawaiian sugar plantation, and running his own fruit and nursery business in Milwaukie, Oregon. U'ren finally settled in Portland, Oregon and opened up a small law practice.

However, he was strongly drawn to the idea of citizens becoming involved in governmental issues in order to make a difference and he dedicated most of his life to that goal. While actually serving one term in the Oregon legislature during 1896-97, he was mostly involved with several populist organizations including the National Popular Government League; the Direct Primary Nominations League; the Anti-Monopoly League; and the People's Power League. He was also secretary of both the Oregon Single Tax League and the Direct Legislation League, and was on the board of directors of the People's Lobby in Washington, D.C.

Through his hard work and effort, the State of Oregon was the first state to elect U.S. Senators popularly chosen by the electorate. Proving that U'ren was ahead of his time, this format was eventually put into law as the Seventeenth Amendment to the Constitution in 1913. Other states paid attention to his ideas as well and adopted many of them. Other reforms created by U'ren include amendment of the state constitution by popular vote and passage of a state corrupt-practices act, as well as having more governmental say-so by way of initiative and referendum, and recall.

William U'ren was married to Mary Beharrell. He died on March 9, 1949.

135

V

VAN SCHAICK, (1817-1901) Isaac Whitbeck (uncle of Aaron Van Schaick Cochrane), a U. S. Representative from Wisconsin; born in Coxsackie, Greene County, N.Y., December 7, 1817; attended the common schools; engaged extensively in the manufacture of glue; moved to Chicago in 1857, and to Wisconsin in 1861 and engaged in the flour-milling business in Milwaukee; elected to the Milwaukee Common Council in 1871; member of the State assembly 1873-1875; served in the State senate 1877- 1882; elected as a Republican to the Forty-ninth Congress (March 4, 1885-March 3, 1887); declined to be a candidate for renomination in 1886; elected to the Fifty-first Congress (March 4, 1889-March 3, 1891); was not a candidate for renomination in 1890; unsuccessful candidate for State senator in 1890; moved to Catonsville, Baltimore County, Md., in 1894, where he lived in retirement until his death there August 22, 1901; interment in Athens Cemetery, Athens,N.Y.

VEBLEN, THORSTEIN BUNDE (1857-1929) was an American economist.

Born on a farm in Manitowoc County, Wisconsin on July 30, 1857, he graduated from Carleton College in 1880. He continued his graduate studies at Johns Hopkins University, later transferring to Yale where he received a Ph.D. degree in 1884.

Initially wanting to be a teacher, he was not able to find any jobs for several years. During the waiting period, he continued to study, eventually deciding to become an economist. In 1891 he enrolled in Cornell University to pursue courses on the subject. When the University of Chicago was established the following year, Veblen became an instructor there, and by 1906, had become an associate professor. That same year he began teaching at Stanford University, and three years later, transferred to the University of Missouri where he taught until 1918.

After the start of World War I, his services were requested in Washington, D.C. as an "industrial aid." However due to his rather abstract and obscure theories, he was sent home. Eventually he moved to New York and began teaching at the New School for Social Research. During that time, he also worked as editor of the *Journal of Political Economy* and *Dial.*

His first book, *The Theory of the Leisure Class,* published in 1899, became a popular treatise on the excesses and foibles of the middle and business classes, and is the original source of the phrase "conspicuous consumption." His other books include: *The Theory of Business Enterprise,* 1904; *The Instinct of Workmanship,* 1914; *Imperial Germany and the Industrial Revolution,* 1915; *An Inquiry into the Nature of Peace,* 1917; *The Higher Learning in America,* 1918; and *The Vested Interests and the State of the Industrial Arts,* 1919; among others.

There were also several books written about him, such as: *Thorstein Veblen and his America,* by Joseph Dorfman (1934); *Thorstein Veblen, A Critical Interpretation,* by David Riesman (1953); and *Veblenism: A New Critique,* by Lev. E. Dobriansky (1958); among others.

Veblen's personal life was a tumultuous one with the writer often having to seek new employment after his entanglements with various women caused the occasional scandal. According to one record, he was married twice.

Thorstein Veblen died on August 3, 1929.

VILAS, WILLIAM FREEMAN, (1840-1908), statesman was born in Chester, Vermont, July 9, 1840, son of Levi B. and Esther G. (Smilie) Vilas. He moved with his family to Madison, Wisconsin and in 1858 graduated from the State University there. The following year he studied at a commercial school and then entered Albany Law School, from which he graduated in 1860.

William Vilas began the practice of his profession in Madison in partnership with Charles T. Wakeley under the firm name of Wakely & Vilas. Eleazer Wakely was admitted to partnership in 1862. Vilas enlisted for the Civil War in July, 1862, and raised Company A of the 23rd Wisconsin regiment which joined Sherman in his expedition against Vicksburg. In Memphis he was stricken with typhoid fever, but after his recovery he rejoined his regiment with which he took part in the campaign of Vicksburg. He was promoted successively to major and lieutenant-colonel; participated in the battles at Port Gibson, Champion Hill, Black River Bridge, and the assaults at Vicksburg, and during nearly all of the siege was in immediate command of his regiment.

Owing to pressing business matters at home, Colonel Vilas resigned in 1864. After the war his practice rapidly increased, and his income secured him in a few years a moderate fortune. From 1872 to 1881 Edwin E. Bryant, later dean of the law faculty of the University of Wisconsin, was his law partner, and for part of this period his brother, Edward P. Vilas, was also a member of the firm.

Subsequent to 1860, Senator Vilas took part on the stump in every political campaign and often represented his district in state conventions. He was a delegate to the national conventions of 1876, 1880, 1884, 1892 and 1896 and was permanent chairman of the convention of 1884. From 1876 to 1886 he was Wiconsin member of the National Committee from 1876-86. In the famous campaign of 1884 Vilas was elected to the State Legislature with little opposition.

Upon the organization of the Cleveland cabinet in 1885 Vilas became Postmaster-General, serving until 1888, when he was appointed Secretary of the Interior to succeed Secretary Lamar, who had been appointed to the Supreme Court of the United States. In the Post Office Department the distinguishing features of his service were the establishment of improved business methods, a reduction in costs with a large increase of service, the complete revision of the postal laws and regulations, the increased expedition of overland mails, and the improvement of the foreign mail services.

The business of the Interior Department was mostly in arrears when Secretary Vilas took charge of it, and he began to relieve those having affairs so involved by working off the accumulations, and by introducing better modes of consideration in the law division. During his incumbency he decided as many land appeals as had been disposed of in the previous four years.

At the end of the Cleveland administration Vilas returned to his law practice in Madison. During the state campaign of 1890 he spoke daily for several weeks at many different points. The result of the election enabled the Democrats to choose, after thirty-five years' interruption, a U.S. senator, in the caucus of 85 votes Vilas received unanimous endorsements on the first ballot. He was formally elected by the Legislature for the six-year term beginning March 4, 1891. In 1896 he refused to support the platform adopted by the convention in Chicago; attended the convention in Indianapolis as a delegate; was chair-

man of the Committee of Resolutions, and was prominent-
ly concerned in the preparation of the platform then
adopted.

Colonel Vilas was a trustee of the Soldiers' Orphans'
Home of Wisconsin and vice-president of the State
Historical Society. He was a devoted member of the Society
of the Army of the Tennessee, and as such gave to this
association his best oratorical efforts. In all the positions he
held throughout his career Senator Vilas applied himself to
the fulfillment of duty with energy, faith, and duty. This
characteristic ran through all his life and illuminated all
his work. Colonel Vilas was married in Madison, Wisconsin, January 3, 1866, to Anna M. Fox, of Fitchburg,
Wisconsin. She survived him with one child, Mary Esther.
Vilas died at Madison, Wisconsin, August 27, 1908.

WALSH, THOMAS JAMES (1859-1933) was a United States Senator.

Born in Two Rivers, Wisconsin on June 12, 1859, he was a high school principal before deciding to pursue law as a career. After attending the University of Wisconsin, he earned a law degree in 1884.

He immediately opened a law practice with his brother Henry in Redfield, South Dakota, and later moved to Helena, Montana in 1890. In 1912, he ran for the U.S. Senate and was elected on the Democratic ticket. An ardent liberal who believed in putting public needs above those of the government, he backed President Woodrow Wilson on the latter's domestic and foreign programs, such as the nomination of Louis D. Brandeis as a Supreme Court Justice, and the inclusion of the United States into the League of Nations. He also helped with the drafting of the 1914 Clayton Act.

Perhaps his greatest contribution to his constituents was his participation in the extensive investigation into the oil lease scandal during Warren G. Harding's administration. After a year and a half of sifting through a vast amount of evidence, Walsh's hard work paid off in the form of the bribery conviction of Secretary of the Interior Albert B. Fall, who was sent to prison for his crimes.

In 1924, Walsh attempted a bid for the presidency but lost to John W. Davis. He continued his Senatorial duties until 1933 when he was named attorney general by President Franklin D. Roosevelt. However, on March 2, two days before the new administration was to take office, Walsh died. He was married to Elinor C. McClements who had died in 1917.

WASIELEWSKI, THADDEUS FRANCIS BOLESLAW, (1904-1976) a U. S. Representative from Wisconsin; born in Milwaukee, Wis., December 2, 1904; attended the parochial schools and South Division High School of his native city; B.A., University of Michigan at Ann Arbor, 1927, and from the law department of Marquette University, Milwaukee,

Wis., J.D., 1931; was admitted to the bar in 1931 and commenced practice in Milwaukee, Wis.; served as census supervisor in 1940; elected as a Democrat to the Seventy-seventh and to the two succeeding Congresses (January 3, 1941-January 3, 1947); unsuccessful Democratic candidate for renomination in 1946 and an unsuccessful Independent candidate for election in 1946 to the Eightieth Congress; delegate, Democratic National Convention, 1948; member, Wisconsin State Central Committee, 1942-1948; resumed the practice of law; resided in Milwaukee, Wis., where he died April 25, 1976; interment in St. Adalbert's Cemetery.

WASSERMAN, DALE (1917-?) mostly known as a playwright, has been involved in several aspects of the entertainment business including work as a lighting designer, producer, director, and writer for stage, screen and television.

Born in Rhinelander, Wisconsin on November 2, 1917, he produced his first Off-Broadway play in 1955 entitled *Livin' the Life* (co-written with Bruce Geller). His other stage works include: *The Pencil of God*, 1961; *998*, 1966; *One Flew Over the Cuckoo's Nest* (adapted from the Ken Kesey novel), 1963; *Man of La Mancha*, 1965, for which he won a Tony Award, and which, for a time, was the third-longest running musical in the history of New York theatre; *Play with Fire*, 1978; *Great Big River*, 1981; and *Shakespeare and The Indians*, 1983.

Some of his screenplays are: *World of Strangers*, 1954; *The Vikings*, 1955; *Two Faces to Go*, 1959; *Cleopatra*, 1963; *Quick, Before It Melts*, 1964; *A Walk with Love and Death*, 1969; and *Man of La Mancha*, 1972.

Wasserman has an extensive list of television credits, some of which include: *Elisha and the Long Knives*, 1954; *The Fog*, 1957; *Eichmann*, 1958; *I, Don Quixote*, 1959; *The Power and the Glory*, 1960; and *The Lincoln Murder Case*, 1961; *Burden of Proof*, 1976; *Scheherazade*, 1977; *The Seventh Dimension*, 1984; *My Name is Esther*, 1985; *The Whole Truth*, 1987; and *A Fine American Family*, 1988; among numerous others.

Wasserman is the founder and artistic director of the Midwest Professional Playwrights Lab, as well as a founding member of the Eugene O'Neill Theatre Center. He has also been a contributor to various periodicals such as *Argosy*, *Redbook*, *True*, *Variety* and the New York *Times*.

Wasserman is married to actress Ramsay Ames.

WEISSE, CHARLES HERMAN, (1866-1919) a U. S. Representative from Wisconsin; born near Sheboygan Falls, Sheboygan County, Wis., October 24, 1866; attended the public schools and St. Paul Lutheran School; in 1880 started to work in a tannery and became a partner in 1888; president of the city council of Sheboygan Falls, Wis., 1893-1896; treasurer of the school board 1897-1900; delegate to the Democratic National Conventions in 1904 and 1908; unsuccessful Democratic candidate for election in 1900 to the Fifty-seventh Congress; elected as a Democrat to the Fifty-Eighth and to the three succeeding Congresses (March 4, 1903-March 3, 1911); was not a candidate for renomination in 1910 to the Sixty-second Congress; engaged in the manufacture of leather and in various other business enterprises in his native city; accidentally killed in Sheboygan Falls, Wis., October 8, 1919; interment in Falls Cemetery.

WELLES, (GEORGE) ORSON (1915-1985) was a child prodigy who was best known for his "ahead-of-its-time" film masterpiece, *Citizen Kane.*

Born in Kenosha, Wisconsin on May 6, 1915, Welles was a brilliant child who reportedly could read by the age of two and could play Igor Stravinsky's music on the violin at the age of seven.

Losing his mother when he was eight and his father when he was thirteen, Welles was taken in by a physician, Dr. Maurice Bernstein. After receiving his education at the Todd School for Boys, Wells refused to pursue a college education and instead, left home to study at the Art Institute of Chicago. In 1931, Welles headed for Ireland, touring the countryside in a donkey-pulled cart. He settled in Dublin and tried to convince the owners of the Gate Theatre that he was an established theatre star in New York. While they didn't believe his story, they were impressed enough by his deep voice and his imposing manner to hire him for the role of the evil Duke of Wurtemberg in *Jew Suss.*

After appearing in a few more roles, Welles returned to New York, then decided to travel once again, going to Morocco and Spain. It was in the latter country that Welles acquired his love for bullfighting and actually participated in the event as a picador.

Returning home in 1933, Welles became a member of Katharine Cornell's acting troupe, playing Mercutio in *Romeo and Juliet.* He later performed in the same play when it reached Broadway, this time playing the role of Tybalt, as well as being part of the Chorus.

During that time, he was also involved in the new medium of radio, playing the role of McGafferty in *Panic*, a work written by Archibald McLeish. He continued his radio work in such shows as NBC's *March of Time* series and became very popular, due to what one observer described as his "splendid purple-velvet voice."

With good friend John Houseman, Welles continued his involvement in the theatre, acting as co-director for the Negro People's Theater under the aegis of the Federal Theatre Project. The two men produced an all-Black version of *Macbeth* at a theatre in Harlem and the show was an overwhelming success.

After doing their next project, *Dr. Faustus*, they experienced some problems when they tried to perform what was considered an anti-capitalist play, *The Cradle Will Rock*. On opening night, both the actors and the audience were locked out of the Maxine Elliot Theatre. Not about to be intimidated, Welles led some 2,000 people up Sixth Avenue to another theater and after seating the crowd, he put on his performance.

In 1937, Houseman and Welles became partners in the Mercury Theatre, an acting troupe that would soon become famous when they performed the radio broadcast of *The War of the Worlds*. In the beginning, they group performed such plays as *Julius Caesar, Shoemaker's Holiday, Heartbreak House* and *Danton's Death*.

During the time that Welles was appearing on CBS's *The Shadow*, he was able to convince the network to hire the Mercury players to perform plays that were adapted from various novels. One of the novels they presented was *The War of the Worlds* by H.G. Wells. The Mercury actors made history on October 30, 1938, when, even after warning listeners before each segment that what they were hearing was fiction, they created a panic across America unheard of before or since. It was Welles' idea to make the story sound as if a Martian invasion was in progress, and the subsequent hysteria caused listeners to do everything from evacuate their homes, pray in the streets, or volunteer for the National Guard.

Eventually the Mercury Theatre could no longer sustain itself financially, and Welles, along with many of the Mercury players, headed for Hollywood and signed with RKO Studios. The work that Welles had previously been involved in was impressive enough that the studio gave him almost total control over the film he was embarking on.

143

He hired many of the Mercury actors including Joseph Cotten, Agnes Moorehead, Everett Sloane, and Ruth Warrick, who was to play his wife in his movie, *Citizen Kane.*

The movie, reportedly based on newspaper magnate William Randolph Hearst, would in later years come to be considered a classic. Both Welles and Herman Mankiewicz won an Academy Award for the screenplay and Welles was also given nominations for best actor and best director. In addition, he is credited (along with his cameraman Gregg Toland) with creating innovative camera techniques such as deep-focus photography and the wide-angle shot. Although at the time of its release it was not an overwhelming box office success, it grew in stature as the years went on and in the 1960's a group of foreign film critics named *Citizen Kane* "the best film in motion picture history."

He continued to be involved with numerous films in some capacity, including: *The Magnificent Ambersons,* as writer/director, 1942; *Journey into Fear,* 1942; *The Lady from Shanghai,* as star and director, 1947; *Prince of Foxes,* 1949; *The Third Man,* 1949; *The Black Rose,* 1950; *Moby Dick,* 1956; *The Long Hot Summer,* 1958; *Compulsion,* 1959; *A Man For All Seasons,* 1966; *Casino Royale,* 1967; *Start the Revolution Without Me,* 1969; *Catch 22,* 1970; *Voyage of the Damned,* 1976; and *The Muppet Movie,* 1979.

It's been pointed out through the years that Welles had conquered radio, theater and films by the time he was twenty-six and had no where to go but down. In his later years he was plagued by insecurity, boredom, and his inability to get the funds he needed for his projects. However, what he did contribute in those early years was impressive, and in 1970, he was given a special Academy Award for "superlative artistry and versatility in the creation of motion pictures." In 1975, the American Film Institute honored Welles with a Lifetime Achievement Award, and in 1984, the Director's Guild bestowed him with their highest honor, the D.W. Griffith Award.

Welles was married three times: to Virginia Nicholson, then to actress Rita Hayworth, and finally to Italian actress Paola Mori. The actor had one daughter from each of his marriages.

Orson Welles died on October 10, 1985.

WESCOTT, GLENWAY (1901-1987) was an author of poetry, fiction and non-fiction, the latter concerning his own childhood.

Born in Kewaskum, Wisconsin on April 11, 1901, he attended the University of Chicago from 1917 to 1919.

Wescott lived abroad in such countries as France, Mexico and Germany between the years 1925 to 1933. Taking up writing full-time in 1921, he had his first work, a book of poems entitled *Bitterns*, published in 1920. He published one more book of poems in 1925 called *Natives of Rock*.

His novels include: *The Apple of the Eye*, 1924; *The Grandmothers: A Family Portrait*, 1927; and *Apartment in Athens*, 1945. His other writings are: *Good-bye Wisconsin* (stories), 1928; *The Babe's Bed* (novella), 1930; *Fear and Trembling* (essays), 1932; *A Calendar of Saints for Unbelievers* (hagiography), 1932; and *The Pilgrim Hawk* (novella), 1940.

He was also the editor and author of the introductions for two works: *The Maugham Reader*, 1950; and *Short Novels of Colette*, 1951. Wescott's last two published works were: a collection of his non-fiction entitled *Images of Truth: Remembrances and Criticism*, 1962; and *The Best of All Possible Worlds: Journals, Letters, and Remembrances, 1914-1937*, 1975.

He also contributed his work to numerous periodicals, including: *Atlantic* ; *Commonweal* ; *Dial* ; *Nation* ; *New Yorker* ; *Saturday Review* ; and *Time*.

Wescott died on February 11, 1987.

WILCOX, ELLA WHEELER (1850-1919), poet and journalist, was born in Johnstown Center, Wisconsin. She attended public schools in nearby Windsor and the the Woman's College of the University of Wisconsin. Most of her education, however, came from the many books she read as a child. Her interest in reading led her into popular literature such as the works of Mary Jane Holmes and Ouida. "I do not remember when I did not expect to be a writer, and I was a neighborhood celebrity at the age of eight," she said. She first published verse in the New York *Mercury* when she was only fourteen and soon gained recognition from that city's publishers when her poems began to appear in *Waverly Magazine* and *Leslie's Weekly*.

In 1872 she wrote her first book, a collection of verses against intemperance, entitled *Drops of Water*, and the same year she wrote *Shells*, a moral and religious collection of poems. Her sentimental and romantic nature was demonstrated in such poems as "Maurine" and *Poems of Passion*, a collection of love verses. A Chicago publisher had rejected the *Poems* on the grounds that they were immoral, but when another publisher released the book in 1883, the rumors of its supposed raciness only served to ensure its success. When 60,000 copies were sold within two years, Ella Wheeler's reputation was made. She lived with her husband, a businessman, in Connecticut until 1887, during which time she wrote *Mal Moulee,* a novel, and *An Ambitious Man.* While living in New York City, she wrote *Men, Women and Emotions* (1893), and a series of poetry collections on *Power, Pleasure, Sentiment,* and *Progress* (1888-1909).

Critics generally found Ella Wheeler Wilcox's verse lofty and full of easy moral truths, but as a *Nation* reviewer wrote: "When Miss Wheeler writes simply and calmly, keeping on her own ground of life and experience, she is strong." After her husband died in 1916, Ms. Wilcox tried to contact his spirit through a series of columns she wrote. She began a lecture tour in Allied Army camps in France, which she said was done under her husband's direction. That same year, she wrote *The Worlds and I.* Early in 1919 she fell ill and quit writing. She died at home in Short Beach, Connecticut later that year.

WILDER, GENE (1934-), born Jerry Silberman, is a comic actor who has starred in, as well as written and directed, numerous films.

Born in Milwaukee, Wisconsin on June 11, 1935, he received a B.A. degree from the University of Iowa in 1955. He then went to England to attend the Bristol Old Vic Theatre School for a year.

He appeared on Broadway in 1962 in the play *The Complaisant Lover,* winning the Clarence Derwent award. He began his film career in 1966 with an appearance in *Bonnie and Clyde.* He has worked steadily in films since then in such movies as: *The Producers,* 1967 (receiving an Academy Award nomination); *Start the Revolution Without Me,* 1968; *Quackser Fortune Has a Cousin in the Bronx,* 1969; *Willy Wonka and the Chocolate Factory,* 1970; *Everything You Always Wanted to Know About Sex,* 1971; *Blazing Saddles,* 1973; *Silver Streak,* 1976; *The Frisco Kid,* 1979; *Stir Crazy,* 1980; and *Hanky Panky,* 1982.

Wilder has also made a number of films where he has been either the actor and/or writer/director: *Young Frankenstein,* 1974 (receiving an Academy Award nomination); *The Adventures of Sherlock Holmes' Smarter Brother,* 1975; *The World's Greatest Lover,* 1977; *Sunday*

Lovers, 1980; *The Woman in Red*, 1984; and *Haunted Honeymoon*, 1986.

During the 1970's he did some television work, including: *The Scarecrow*, 1972; *The Trouble With People*, 1973; *Marlo Thomas Special*, 1973; and *Thursday's Games*, 1973.

Wilder has been married twice--to Mary Joan Schutz whom he divorced in 1974, and comedienne Gilda Radner who died of cancer. He has one daughter from his first marriage.

WILDER, LAURA INGALLS (1867-1957) was an author who was best known for her *Little House* series.

Born in Lake Pepin, Wisconsin on February 7, 1867, she lived in the Midwest, mainly in the Dakota Territory, and most of her books are an autobiographical account of those years. However, she was sixty-five before she began writing her popular books.

Wilder taught school for many years, was the editor of the *Missouri Ruralist*, and had many of her stories published in magazines. Beginning in 1932, she wrote the first of her many books about life on the frontier, entitled *Little House in the Big Woods*. Her subsequent editions were *Farmer Boy*, 1933; *Little House on the Prairie*, 1935; *On the Banks of Plum Creek*, 1937; *By the Shores of Silver Lake*, 1939; *The Long Winter*, 1940; *Little Town on the Prairie*, 1941; and *These Happy Golden Years*, 1943.

She married Almanzo J. Wilder in 1885 and they had one daughter. Laura Ingalls Wilder died on January 10, 1957.

WILDER, THORNTON (1897-1975), playwright and novelist, was born April 17, 1897 in Madison, Wisconsin, the son of Amos and Isabella (Niven) Wilder. His father was named American Consul General in 1906 and the family moved to Hong Kong. After a few months there, however, Thornton's mother took him and his brother and sisters back to the United States, and they lived in Berkeley, California for the next five years. In 1911 they Amos Wilder in Shanghai for a year, then returned to California where Thornton completed his early education at Thacher School in Ojai, and then at Berkeley High School. He became interested in writing and theater while in high school, and had his first prose pieces published in the school literary magazine while attending Oberlin College from 1915 to 1917. He transferred to Yale, where he had more works published, including his first full-length play, *The Trumpet Shall Sound.* During World War I, he served as a corporal in the Coast Guard artillery, and following the war he returned to Yale and completed his B.A. in 1920.

Wilder then went to Rome to study archaeology at the American Academy. During his year in Italy, he started his first novel, *The Cabala,* published in 1926. From 1921 to 1928 he taught French at Lawrenceville School in New Jersey, meanwhile working toward his M.A. in French literature, which he received at Princeton University in 1926. From 1930 to 1936 he was a lecturer of comparative literature at the University of Chicago. While teaching, Wilder also continued to write. His play, *The Trumpet Shall Sound* was produced in New York in 1927 to small comment. However that same year, he was catapulted to international fame with the release of his novel, *The Bridge of San Luis Rey.* The book, which told the story of the lives of five individuals killed when a bridge collapsed in Peru, and pondered the questions of fate, love, and the meaning of death, won the 1928 Pulitzer Prize for fiction and quickly became a best-seller.

Wilder followed this novel in 1930 with *The Women of Andros,* and in 1935 with *Heaven's My Destination.* He also continued to work as a playwright, creating a number of short plays which were compiled in the books, *The Angel That Troubled the Waters* (1928) and *The Long Christmas Dinner and Other Plays in One Act* (1931). His full-length plays were collected in 1957 in *Three Plays,* published by Harper. Wilder received a Pulitzer Prize in drama for his 1938 play, *Our Town,* produced at the Henry Miller Theatre on Broadway. The play caught the eye of the critics in part because of its staging with no scenery and only the barest props—an innovation of Wilder and producer Jed Harris.

Later that same year, Wilder's comedic play, *The Merchant of Yonkers, A Farce in Four Acts* closed after a mere 28 performances. In 1942, however, he staged a comeback with his play, *The Skin of Our Teeth,* his second work of theater to win a Pulitzer Prize. Wilder took a three year break during World War II to serve in the U.S. Army Intelligence, where he rose to the rank of lieutenant colonel. His works after the war included: the novels, *The Ides of March* (1948), and *The Eighth Day* (1967), which won the National Book Award of 1968; and the play, *The Matchmaker* which was adapted into the musical, *Hello Dolly* in 1964. In 1965, at a White House ceremony, he became the first to receive the National Book Committee's National Medal for Literature. Wilder died in Hamden, Connecticut on December 7, 1975.

WILEY, ALEXANDER, (1884- 1967) a U. S. Senator from Wisconsin; born in Chippewa Falls, Chippewa County, Wis., May 26, 1884; attended the public schools, Augsburg College, Minneapolis, Minn., and the University of Michigan at Ann Arbor; graduated from the law department of the University of Wisconsin at Madison in 1 907; was admitted to the bar the same year and commenced practice in Chippewa Falls, Wis.; district attorney of Chippewa County 1909-1915; unsuccessful Republican candidate for governor in 1936; engaged in agricultural pursuits and banking; elected as a Republican to the United States Senate in 1938; reelected in 1944, 1950, and again in 1956, and served from January 3, 1939, to January 3, 1963; unsuccessful candidate for reelection in 1962; chairman, Committee on the Judiciary (Eightieth Congress), Committee on Foreign Relations (Eighty-third Congress), resided in Washington, D.C., until a few days before his death, May 26, 1967, at High Oaks Christian Science Church Sanitarium in Germantown, Pa.; interment in Forest Hill Cemetery, Chippewa Falls, Wis.

WINANS, JOHN, (1831-1907) a U. S. Representative from Wisconsin; born in Vernon, Sussex County, N.J., September 27, 1831; studied law and was admitted to the bar in 1855; moved to Janesville, Rock County, Wis., in 1857 and practiced his profes-sion; member of the board of aldermen of Janesville in 1861; city attorney 1865-1875; member of the State assembly in 1874, 1882, 1887, and 1891; delegate to the Democratic National Convention in 1864; served as colonel on the staff of Governor Taylor in 1874 and 1875; mayor of Janesville 18851 887; elected as a Democrat to the Forty-eighth Congress (March 4, 1883-March 3, 1885); was not a candidate for renomination in 1884; engaged in the practice of law in Janesville, Wis., until his death January 17, 1907; interment in Oak Hill Cemetery.

WITHROW, GARDNER ROBERT, (1892-1964) a U. S. Representative from Wisconsin; born in La Crosse, Wis., October 5, 1892; attended the grade and high schools; after two years of legal training engaged in railroading as a fireman and conductor 1912-1931; member of the Wisconsin assembly in 1926 and 1927; served as State representative for the railroad brotherhoods 1928-1931; elected as a Republican to the Seventy-second and Seventy-third Congresses and as a Progressive to the Seventy-fourth and Seventy-fifth Congresses (March 4, 1931-January 3, 1939); unsuccessful candidate for reelection in 1938 to the Seventy-sixth Congress, and for election in 1940 to the Seventy-seventh Congress and in 1942 to the Seventy-eighth Congress; resumed activities as State representative for the Brotherhood of Railroad Trainmen; elected as a Republican to the Eighty-first and to the five succeeding Congresses (January 3, 1949-January 3, 1961); did not seek renomination in 1960; was a resident of La Crosse, Wis., until his death September 23, 1964; interment in Oak Grove Cemetery.

WOODWARD, GILBERT MOTIER, (1835- 1913) a U. S. Representative from Wisconsin; born in Washington, D.C., December 25, 1835; educated in the common schools; studied law; was admitted to the bar in 1861 and commenced practice in La Crosse, Wis., in February 1860; served more than three years in the Union Army during the Civil War as a private, first sergeant, second lieutenant, first lieutenant, and adjutant in the Second Regiment, Wisconsin Volunteer Infantry; district attorney of La Crosse County 1866-1873; mayor of the city of La Crosse in 1874 and 1875; city attorney 1876-1882; elected as a Democrat to the Forty-eighth Congress (March 4, 1883) March 3, 1885); unsuccessful for reelection in 1884 to the Forty-ninth Congress; resumed the practice of law in La Crosse, Wis.; unsuccessful Democratic candidate for Governor of Wisconsin in 1886; delegate to the Democratic National Convention in 1888; died in La Crosse, Wis., March 13, 1913; interment in Oak Grove Cemetery.

WRIGHT, FRANK LLOYD (1869-1959), architect, was born in Richland Center, Wisconsin on June 8, 1869, the son of William and Anna Lloyd (Jones) Wright. His mother encouraged him to become an architect, and in 1884 he enrolled at the University of Wisconsin as a civil engineering student (the university didn't offer a course in architecture). Wright studied for three years, then went to Chicago and worked as a draftsman with architect, J. L. Silsbee. It was there he designed a house for his aunts in Spring Green, Wisconsin—his first executed work.
    In 1888 he took a five-year position as a designer with the prominent architectural firm of Denkmar Adler and Louis Sullivan. The following year he married Catherine Lee Clark Tobin. Wright left Adler and Sullivan in 1893 to

work independently. During this time he designed several Chicago houses; the watertower and wooden windmill in Spring Green; and the Golf Club and the Winslow House in River Forest. He was widely recognized for his innovative "Prairie house" design in 1900, with windows grouped in long rows and rooms that flowed into one another. Between 1902 and 1909 he built a number of Prairie-style houses in the Chicago area. Also notable during this period were his designs for the Larkin Company's Administration Building in Buffalo (1904), which included air-conditioning, all-metal furniture, and was the first in the U.S. to use metal-bound plate-glass doors and windows; and for The Unity Temple Church in Oak Park (1906).

In 1910, after a portfolio of Wright's designs was published in Berlin, he began to exert an influence on the new modern architects of Europe. Wright completed a number of important works in the years that followed: Midway Gardens (1914), an open-air casino in Chicago that used abstract painting and sculpture in its ornamentation; the famous Imperial Hotel of Tokyo (1922), using cantilevered floors and a foundation on a cushion of mud to make it earthquake proof (the hotel proved its fine architectural engineering in 1923 when it rode out a devastating quake without damage); the Millard House of Pasadena (1923), the first to use Wright's concrete block reinforced with metal strips method of construction.

With the coming of the Great Depression, many of Wright's commissions dried up. He turned to writing and spent much of his time giving lectures across the country. Meanwhile, he and wife, Catherine divorced, and in 1922 he wed Miriam Noel, a marriage that lasted until 1927. In 1928 he married Olga Lazovich, of Montenegro. With the revival of construction in the mid-1930s, Wright received new work. He designed the Kaufmann House of Bear Run, Pennsylvania (1936), cantilevered over a waterfall, noted by his critics as one of his most beautiful architectural works. Other designs included the Johnson Wax Administration building in Racine, Wisconsin (1939), with its well-known mushroom-shaped columns inside, and an exterior incorporating brick and horizontal glass tubing; the Herbert Jacobs House near Madison (1937), the first of Wright's Usionian houses; the Herbert Jacobs House II (1942), known for its crescent shape; the V. C. Morris Gift Shop in San Francisco (1949) with its simple bare brick facade; the Friedman House near Pleasantville, New York (1951), with its circular design; the fifteen-floor Johnson Wax Research and Development building (1950); the

Solomon R. Guggenheim Museum in New York (1959); and the campus of Florida Southern College in Lakewood.

Frank Lloyd Wright wrote numerous books. He was hailed as the greatest architect of the twentieth century and received many awards and honorary degrees for excellence in architecture. He had seven children. He died April 9, 1959.

Z

ZIMMERMAN, FRED R. (1880-1954), twenty-fifth governor of Wisconsin, was born on November 20,1880 in Milwaukee, the son of Charles and Augusta (Fiesenhauser) Zimmerman. His father died when he was five, and he worked as a child to help support the family. He finished grammar school, and for a short time attended night school. In 1902, he became a milkman for the Bee Hive Dairy in Milwaukee. He married Amanda Freedy in 1904. They had two sons.

Zimmerman held a series of jobs over the next several years, including work as a salesman, bookkeeper, and head of his own business, Berthlet & Company, which sold building materials. He entered politics in 1908 when he ran for the Wisconsin Assembly and won by six votes. Between 1912 and 1915, he was a board member for the town of Lake. He became director of industrial relations for Nash Motor Company in 1920. Two years later his political career continued when he was elected Secretary of State. He served two terms, and in 1926 ran for governor on the Republican ticket, winning over Independent Charles B. Perry and Democrat Virgil H. Cady. Zimmerman's administration was marked by the passage of the first drivers' license law in Wisconsin, the establishment of a system for permanent voter registration in cities of over 5,000, the creation of a six-man conservation commission, and modifications to income tax.

Zimmerman ran for governor once again in 1928, but finished third in the primary. In 1929, President Hoover named him envoy to the Spanish-American Exposition in Seville, Spain. He returned to Wisconsin and ran for governor in 1934, losing again in the primary. From 1935 to 1936 he was a certifying officer for the Works Progress Administration. He ran an unsuccessful race for Congress in 1936. Two years later he helped establish the firm Better Properties, Inc. of Milwaukee, and became its president. That same year he was elected Secretary of State, a post he held for nine consecutive terms. He tried unsuccessfully for a seat on the Supreme Court in 1945. Fred Zimmerman died on December 14, 1954.

Index to Persons

156

Prairie View Elementary
W330 S6473 Highway E
North Prairie, WI 53153